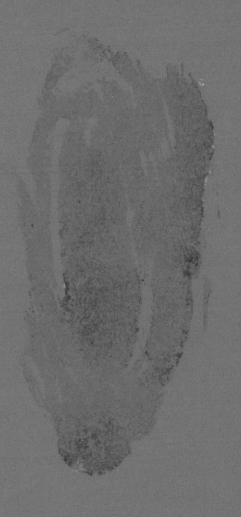

TONIGHT!

Also by Terry Galanoy

DOWN THE TUBE

Terry Galanoy

* * * * * * * * * * * * * * * * *

TONIGHT!

Doubleday & Company, Inc.
Garden City, New York
1972

ISBN: 0-385-02882-2
Library of Congress Catalog Card Number 72–76159
Copyright © 1972 by Terry Galanoy
All Rights Reserved
Printed in the United States of America
First Edition

This book is about talking and is dedicated to Hollyhart, Heather and Hilary, who refrained from a lot of same while it was being written

A couple of years ago I wrote a book called *Down the Tube* and it landed me on the *Tonight Show—starring Johnny Carson* for five months and twelve minutes. The twelve minutes I spent out in the spotlights. The five months I spent deep in the background —of America's favorite television show. What I found, on stage and backstage, is all here.

In tracking down almost twenty years of shows and tens of thousands of guests and the hundreds of people who worked with one or both, I needed the best help I could get. For a great deal of the Steve Allen material, I am grateful to Donna Zink and to Steve Allen's swift and terrifyingly efficient staff. Mort Werner, the longtime programming boss at the National Broadcasting Company opened his memories and his press files to me, and for those absolutely essential favors I thank him and them. I also owe a large debt of gratitude (plus, I think, some more money) to Alison Echavarria, a spectacularly talented researcher who knows how to look up lines in a book or get ahead of them at the copying machines. And I would like to thank those who shall remain nameless—by popular demand—for taking me behind the scenes and giving me information known only to the inside groups. And finally, I would like to thank Fran Collin and Julie Coopersmith for pulling this book all together and Marilyn Galanoy for doing the same for the writer.

T.G.
Newport Beach, California

"We will go into outer space from Mount Palomar; we will follow the electron microscope into the brain; we will attend history wherever it is being made; our people will meet the great personalities of their time face to face, not in a formal presentation but in informal conversations where you really get a feeling of the innate personality."

Sylvester L. Weaver, President, NBC
London, September 27, 1955

☆ **1**

Millions and millions of Americans (you?) do two things late at night. They take something off and they put something on. What they take off is a miracle of our times, permanent press. What they put on is the *Tonight Show,* another miracle of our times because of its permanent presence.

Last night, the night before that, six nights a week, fifty-two weeks a year, anywhere from two to twelve million people have tuned in to this national mouth marathon. Through some twenty years of thick commercials and thin intellectualism, and through four RCA TK-44 cameras, the *Tonight Show* has become the most widely witnessed single event in the history of the world.

Under seven different names and formats, the *Tonight Show* has reached a combined total of more people than all the wars, all the famines, all the rock festivals, all the coronations, the football games, white sales, all the Crusades, pilgrimages to Mecca and all the people in all the public transportation at five o'clock everywhere even including the Holland Tunnel.

Today, or rather, tonight, the show is transmitted to over two hundred and twenty television stations covering over ninety-nine percent of this nation including Alaska and Hawaii. That's better coverage than the telephone companies can offer, the electric companies can boast, than even McDonald's hamburger stands can muster up.

On a fairly good night the show is watched by one and a half people in close to eight million homes. Without even getting their desk-top Dayglo-numeraled computers out, the National Broadcasting Company claims that close to half the homes in this country see the *Tonight Show* four times a month.

That's more people than live in any city in the world or for that matter in any one of forty-four states or ninety-eight foreign countries. It's as if every man, woman and child in New Zealand, Israel, Fiji and Denmark were tuned in at one time.

The *Tonight Show* takes more time out of its viewers' lives than their dinners, their love-making, their exercising, their reading or other recreations.

Has it been worth it? Has the original late night television talk show become the common man's window on the world? Has the microwave relay become his seven-league boots? Has the *Tonight Show* made "the common man into the uncommon man, and mass man into class man" as one NBC visionary dreamed?

Or has it been twenty years of droppings from the sandman down a bottomless hourglass?

You were watching some of the time. What do you think? Did you watch the night Martin Luther King said, "It isn't how long you live but how well you live," just before he went off to be killed?

And did you see Senator Robert Kennedy on that program before he was killed?

Or the President of the United States, John F. Kennedy, in his *Tonight Show* appearances—before he was killed?

Did you watch Dr. Sam Sheppard shock the country by admitting he carried a hidden gun into the courtroom all during his murder trial?

Did you watch when Dr. Paul Ehrlich began changing the country's sexual and breeding habits by saying, "We're going to have to stop having children—before the governments are forced to destroy them"?

Were you watching the night Jack Paar called Ed Sullivan a liar? The night he called Walter Winchell un-American? The night he defied the United States Senate? How about the night he walked out of NBC and his job?

One night Mickey Rooney was thrown off the show for appearing drunk, which was odd because Adam Clayton Powell made many appearances in a questionable state.

Were you watching?

Did you hear Truman Capote upset the nation's jurists with his imprudent jurisprudent comment that it was better to punish the innocent than free the guilty?

How about the time Jerry Lewis cracked, "I fulfilled a lifetime ambition by using the bathroom while flying over Mississippi"?

Did you see the astronauts explain the moon mission exactly the way they reported it to NASA officials?

Did you cry at the lovely, tulip-strewn wedding of Tiny Tim to Miss Vicky? Did you start wearing turtlenecks because Johnny did? Did you go on a water diet, a grapefruit diet, a safflower-oil diet or a liquor diet, like the guest doctors said you should?

Did you help discover Steve Lawrence, Eydie Gorme, Andy Williams, Steve Allen, Dick Gregory, Nipsey Russell,

Carol Burnett, Joan Rivers, Bill Cosby, Flip Wilson, Louis Nye, Dayton Allen, Tom Poston, Bill Dana, Don Knotts and a thousand others—and were you tuned in the night a girl named Barbra Streisand came on the Jack Paar *Tonight Show* for the first time and sang and everything grew very stilled and hushed and respectful all the way from a Philadelphia firehouse to a Lake Superior freighter and from a Chicago locker room to a Honolulu saloon and from a Cedar Rapids jail to a Juneau construction shack?

How about all those other new friends who became old, old chums in a manner of minutes? There was Jerry Lester. Milton DeLugg. Dagmar. Wayne Howell. Jack Paar. Dody Goodman. Geneviève. Charlie Weaver. Gene Rayburn. Jose Melis. Alexander King. Jack Douglas. Jack Lescoulie. Hugh Downs. Skitch Henderson. Johnny Carson. Ed McMahon. Doc Severinsen.

People you spent more time with than you did with a lot of your neighbors.

Did Irving Stone sell you his book, *Lust for Life*, did Erich Segal bore you to tears with his pixieish performances or drive you to same with *Love Story?* Did you buy one of Dr. Stillman's get-rich-quick series of get-thin-quick books? Or David Reuben's ignorance-is-definitely-not-bliss book about sex or alternatives to late night television I have known?

Even products. Look around your house.

The ad agencies brought you some new friends, too. The Polaroid camera. Calgon. Texize. Budweiser beer. Alpo dog food. Sara Lee cakes. Kellogg's cereals. All ringing cash registers the next day through the ringing in your ears the night before.

Pity the poor persons (NBC says maybe ten in a million) who have never seen or heard the *Tonight Show*.

They missed the delights, the laughs, the excitements of Dublin's Mayor Robert Briscoe, Salvador Dali, Ted Kennedy, King Peter, Frank Sinatra, Everett Dirksen, Barry Goldwater, Steve McQueen, Simon and Garfunkel, Judy Garland, Sandy

Koufax, Yael and Mrs. Moshe Dayan, Bishop James Pike, Darryl Zanuck, Lennon and McCartney, Ronald Reagan, Edmund Muskie, Ralph Williams, Richard Nixon, Carl Stokes, Roman Polanski, Christiaan Barnard and all the people who go to the moon or sing a tune or hit a ball or who play three weeks at the Desert Sands, two weekends at the Royal Box, a split week at Harrah's Lake Tahoe.

If they've been heard of outside their home towns, chances are they've been on the *Tonight Show*. Over a thousand guests a year—four or five a night for ten years on the Johnny Carson *Tonight Show* and about that number on the Jack Paar *Tonight Show* and five or six a night on *Tonight! America After Dark* and at least one or two a night during the Steve Allen *Tonight Show* comes to almost twenty thousand of the famous, the fabulous and the freaks who have blabbed, chatted, whispered, shouted, confided, lisped, joked, preached, pleaded, confessed, propositioned and sworn on the *Tonight Show*.

Propositioned and sworn?

Sure.

Out of twenty thousand guests in a live television format, somebody was certain to let loose with language that would turn NBC's studios from an electronic showcase into a combination bawdy and outhouse.

All the four-letter words have been part of the proceedings at one time or another during the twenty years of NBC late night television. Zsa Zsa Gabor, Shelley Winters, dozens of others—even Johnny Carson himself—have had their mouths washed out with bleep brand soap or have been excised completely through the magic of the electronic eraser. The NBC Standards and Practices Department constantly puts their standards in practice and they ride that bleep button like a dead man's switch on the Super Chief. There is a thick, double-locked file of utterances-that-would-befoul-America's-air and NBC's standing with the FCC, under sturdy lock and key. It is just as well it remains a secret. It is not that fascinating. It does nothing for the show, for the guests or even for the audiences to find out that Zsa Zsa can pronounce the slang word for vagina or that David Susskind wanted to do sexual things with Shelley Winters or that members of a satirical group called The Committee knew the street word for sexual intercourse or that Lauren Bacall once lusted after Johnny Carson's body.

The producers say that no one has ever been put on a blacklist for being too outspoken, too frank or too controversial but they lie, or rather, they lie still under the thumb of NBC.

There is a definite list of people, at NBC's Standards and Practices office, who are not welcome on that program. The list can change daily but when this book was being prepared these were the *personae* who were *non grata* at the *Tonight Show:*

You won't have a nice visit with Ralph Nader because this consumer protection leader is not welcome on that show. Too many advertisers can put too much pressure on the network for helping his case, which generally hurts theirs.

Attorney William Kunstler, defender of the Chicago conspiracy group, can go peddle his legal papers elsewhere.

Once in a while Dr. David Reuben, the author of *Everything You Always Wanted to Know About Sex*, etc., isn't invited on. Reuben's frank talk about masturbation, lesbianism, homosexuality—and the naturalness of it all—is still "prevert" talk out in some of middle America.

Christine Jorgensen, who surgically changed sexes, can go tell about her operation elsewhere. So can April Ashley, the man-turned-woman who is now married to an English sailor.

Robert Townsend, author of the best seller, *Up the Organization,* can't come back again. One show was one too many for NBC and its proprietors, the Sarnoff family.

During his appearance on the program Townsend was asked by Johnny Carson if nepotism was a major problem in American industry.

Without a pause, Townsend, ex-head of Avis Rent-A-Car, said yes, it was, that the Fords should have left the car business years ago and that an even better example of nepotism was located right there in the RCA Building.

He said something like, "Nepotism is at its worst right here. I envision every night Robert Sarnoff [Chairman of the Board] picking up one of his children, carrying him over to the window and looking out over Rockefeller Center and saying, 'Someday this will all be yours and you, too, can turn sixty million minds to mush.'"

You probably won't see Tommy and Dickie Smothers do a return engagement because they are so politically and professionally difficult.

Cesar Chavez, the California grape picker and union organizer, can go stomp his grapes of wrath elsewhere.

Mr. Inside Washington columnist Jack Anderson and his past exposures of political kickbacks, the Pentagon papers and Nixon's secret stands is Mr. Outside the *Tonight Show*.

Officials of the ecological Friends of the Earth movement are not considered that friendly.

Dr. Janoff, author of *The Primal Scream*, can scream his head off but he won't get any of Carson's prime(al) time.

Madeleine leRoux, star of *The Dirtiest Show in Town*, is too blue a subject for the azure-tinged *Tonight* crew.

They also don't think that bearded Allen Ginsberg's poetry or soothing transcendental "oms" are exactly what Carson's viewers want.

Tony Curtis hasn't been asked since he was uncovered smoking marijuana and movie director Dennis Hopper is turned down for his public glorification of drugs.

The list, right now, ends with Jane Fonda for her explosive political views and with a few people like Jinx Falkenberg, who took advantage of her visit to promote a cosmetic line instead of promoting the program.

There are other people you haven't seen on the *Tonight Show*, too. Think about it. Rock Hudson hasn't been there or

Greta Garbo or Katharine Hepburn or Marlene Dietrich or Cary Grant on stage, although he once sat in the audience as a joke.

Rock Hudson won't appear because he admits he can't order a sandwich in a restaurant without a script.

Garbo won't show up for a million-dollar part in a film so why should she show up for a $290 walk-on at NBC?

Dietrich won't use her famous legs to do a walk-on.

The show almost landed the elusive Mae West once. That was back in the Steve Allen days. She was willing but the NBC censors weren't. They didn't much care for the way she played her opening line as a Western schoolmarm.

"Hi. My name is Belle," she was supposed to say. "They call me that because of the way I go ding-dong."

"How about June Allyson instead?" the censor suggested, walking away.

That's why you didn't see her.

If you ever wondered who else watches the *Tonight Show* —on the nation's turned-on sixty-two million television sets —NBC spent good money to find out that nine out of ten viewers are adults, that seven out of ten are high school graduates or have more than one year of college, that nearly half of the family heads are white-collar or professional workers and that the Northeastern states are the steadiest, most loyal viewers with twenty-seven percent of their available audience tuned in while the Pacific Coast has only twelve percent watching.

If you've been watching *Tonight*—even just once a year since it came on—then you know that it's been the same but it's been different. Sometimes it seemed that Jerry Lester and Jack Lescoulie and Steve Allen and Jack Paar and Johnny Carson were all interchangeable and sometimes it seemed that only the name was the same but everything else was a foreign-language film.

The first *Tonight* kind of show was called *Broadway Open House* and it had two scurrying hosts, an accordionist and a blonde who blocked cameras with her bust and English grammar with her jokes.

When Steve Allen's *Tonight* came on, so did intelligent comedy, serious writers and controversial problems.

Jack Paar added the sofa and the panel and the non-stop mouths—his and his repeat guests. He was also television's first sob brother.

Johnny Carson kept the best of them, then added his own impish humor and accurate taste for good showmanship.

Back in Jerry Lester's days, a guest with a political opinion would never have been asked back. Today on *Tonight*, a guest without one stands that chance.

"We've talked about narcotics addiction, we've talked about civil rights, and we've talked about liberalizing divorce and abortion laws," Carson says. "But it's all in the way you do it. Some people think controversy is inviting a homosexual on the show and asking him, 'Should we legalize homosexuality?' That's not controversy. That's an obvious attempt to stir up sensation. These things are gimmicks. And afterwards where do you go when you run out of weirdos?"

Did you agree with him when he said that? Or did you find yourself turning to Dick Cavett where the confrontations were? Does Carson just pay short-upper-lip service to important issues?

Except for early *Broadway Open House*, NBC's late night television shows haven't been all laughs. A lot of people think of Carson's *Tonight Show* as an hour and a half of smoker gags. If they watched it, like you do, they'd know that Carson sometimes puts his irony in the fire and attacks old-fashioned venereal disease laws, the telephone company, General Motors, bad plays and parking lots. The one area Carson won't enter is politics. He may have learned a lesson from Jack Paar. Paar, once angry with the then mayor of New York, Robert Wagner, attacked the city administration and the man's mayoral abilities for weeks before the election. As the balloting day grew closer, Paar became more and more outspoken about Wagner and more and more dictatorial about how his audience should vote.

Despite his influence or maybe because of it, Wagner was re-elected.

Carson and his producers try to balance the show but they feel their main destiny is to *entertain* the weary, the drowsy, the bushed, the had-it-for-the-day crowd who don't want to be pummeled about the head with the problems of the world.

He once said, "By eleven-thirty at night the audience has had two major newscasts. The major function of the *Tonight Show* is to entertain. If the audience thought we were going to talk about sociological problems for ninety minutes, the sound of sets turning off all over the country would break your eardrums and our hearts."

So the circle has come full round.

The *Tonight Show* is still laughing it up—after twenty years of late night television. And so are the people associated with it.

Why shouldn't they?

The *Tonight Show* is not only the last word of the broadcasting day, it is the last word in recognition.

The astronauts haven't been anywhere until they've been to Carson's couch.

The All-American football team isn't official until all America has looked them over on *Tonight*.

A standup comic who can get eight minutes on *Tonight* can get two years on the Playboy-Las Vegas-Puerto Rico-Acapulco-Miami Beach tour.

Any political candidate would give up three baby-kissing pictures, an Indian bonnet ceremony and a million "Stick with Me" pins for a shot at NBC's midnight masses.

Scientists slaver and jump with Pavlovian reaction if they have the slightest chance of getting on the show.

Doctors use it to peddle nostrums, cures, nerve tonics,

theories, serums, clinics, diets, vaccines and themselves to the Nobel Committee.

Astrologers and their predictions, actors and their plays, authors and their books, columnists and their insides, ministers with or without their churches, and ecologists who aren't waiting for any grass to grow under their feet because they're sure it won't, all want some of Carson's time.

There was once a man named Pat Weaver at NBC and his dream was to make television the most influential, powerful, beneficial mass communication medium man has ever known. One of his legacies—perhaps the best one—is the *Tonight Show*.

Some say it is just a framework to sell spot remover, soups, bandages, chocolates, aspirins, bread and potato chips.

Some say it is a network moneymaker there only to grind out fifty-five thousand dollars a week for Carson and thirty million a year for NBC.

Some say it is Muzak for the mind, chewing gum for the gray cells, a Seconal for the senses.

And others say it is a stimulating, challenging, educational, idea-exposing, mind-enlarging, growth-promoting experience.

There are good arguments on both sides. Top experts will take the stand—or the seat on Carson's right hand—and testify to either. Every sociologist, behaviorist, educator or national leader has two points of view about it—the one for his colleagues and the other if he has a book he wants to promote on that show.

Tens of millions are the children of NBC's late night television. It has been a definite influence on their ideas, attitudes, outlooks and behavior—like the schools they went to, the people they lived with, the jobs they've held, the loves they've lost, the friends they've enjoyed, the cities in which they've lived, the churches they went to, the wars they fought. Whether the *Tonight Show* has been a good use of waste time or a waste of good time requires all the facts. Where did the *Tonight Show* come from? How did it get there? How did it drive its competition off the tube? What has made it the most witnessed event in the history of the world? And what happened to it along the way to put it in that unique position? It's all in this book.

Is the *Tonight Show* television's finest hour (and a half)?

Or has it made this a nation force-fed with other people's talk while it becomes mute?

Should you just lie there and take more of this?

Or is it time to find your own words and start talking back . . .

. . . to the *Tonight Show*—known sometimes as the monkey on America's pillow-supported back?

2

"The grand design of television," wrote National Broadcasting Company Vice-President Sylvester L. "Pat" Weaver in *Television* magazine, ". . . is to create an aristocracy of the people, the proletariat of privilege, the Athenian masses—to make the average man the uncommon man . . . television will make adults out of children. . . ."

"It will more likely make children out of adults," cracked one newspaper columnist after looking at Weaver's new late night show, *Broadway Open House.*

It was May 1950. With wobbly cameras and firm conviction plus two stars grabbed off at the last minute, the National Broadcasting Company began the first live, all-singing, all-dancing, all-talking late night television show. Although it would change names, faces, places, shapes and ideas for at least the next twenty years, that first late night variety show drastically changed the lives of tens of thousands of people who would appear on later versions of it and the tens of millions who would watch them.

It would change America's sleeping habits, its sex rituals, its radio programs, its music, entertainment, politics, mass communications and even what it ate, drank, drove and took for an upset stomach. It would change the three-million-set television toy into a sixty-million-set monster. It would castrate advertising agencies, would change the way the television men talked to the audience and the way the advertisers paid for the show. Most importantly, it would expose more people to more human ideas, thoughts, theories and platforms than all the books in all the libraries in the country.

Of course, nobody could read all of that between the scanning lines that balmy Monday night in 1950 at eleven o'clock Eastern Standard Time. A red-eyed camera focused on every lighter gray and darker gray light on Broadway, the drummer hit a rim shot backbeat and the hand-lettered slide, BROADWAY OPEN HOUSE, flickered on screen for a second, vanished, then came on and stayed on as boldly as the promises Pat Weaver had made about late night television.

Broadway Open House was planned to be a "lighthearted, zany party-type variety show," according to NBC. It was more like "a heavy-handed, knee-slapping matinee at the burlecue," according to one early watcher. It had two hosts, both short, fast-lipped, vaudeville-wise bananas who dealt out a mixture of old radio gags, four-a-day blackouts, smoker leers and shuffles off to Buffalo in the hopes that was what NBC had wanted. One host was an ex-ballet dancer and night club comic known to some as "The Heckler of Hecklers" and to others as Jerry Lester. Spelling him on Monday and Wednesday nights was a cello-playing wiseacre who was called "radio's greatest egoist" by some of his fans and Morey Amsterdam by others.

Actually, neither one was supposed to have the job. They

were both deadline-minute replacements for a comedian named Don "Creesh" Hornsby.

In line with keeping it "zany and lighthearted," one NBC executive had suggested they build the *Broadway Open House* program about "Creesh" Hornsby.

"What does he do?" someone asked.

"He works in clubs and he, uh, runs around the room yelling, 'Creesh! Creesh!' " was the answer. "You have to see him. It's very funny."

It must have been because the people who decide things like that at NBC decided to entrust their new nighttime opportunity to a man who ran around the room yelling, "Creesh! Creesh!"

Unfortunately for NBC, for *Broadway Open House* and for Don Hornsby, he died suddenly of polio—so suddenly that the producers had only two weeks in which to dig up a replacement. Unearthed and cleaned up in time for the première were Lester and Amsterdam.

Sitting around the "house" as the earliest permanent guests were singers Andy Roberts and Jane Harvey, an announcer named Wayne Howell, an accordionist named Milton De-Lugg and four backup musicians.

They dragged out every proven routine, entrance gag and exit line from the Roxy, Capitol, Paramount, Strand, Oriental, El Tinge, Copa, Latin Quarter, Chez Paree, Flamingo and El Rancho and when they ran out of those they dragged out a "Beanbag" club which viewers could join, a tap dancer named Ray Malone and a gross, malaprop-ridden mountain girl who "boob-trapped" the audience with her 40 D-cup breasts. Her name was Jennie Lewis but they renamed her Dagmar, seated her on a stool at stage front and told her to just sit there and breathe. Later, the writers gave her "dumb blonde" routines to read in a flat monotone. Inflating her chest so it took two cameras to properly cover her, Dagmar said she rode to work on "an ominous bus," that a mushroom was . . . "a place where you made love," that languish was

. . . "human speech," and isolate means . . . "admitting you're tardy." With her strapless gowns, mass of loose-hanging strawberry-blonde hair and an air of uncrackable innocence, Dagmar went from a beginning salary of $75 a week on *Broadway Open House* to $3250 a week when she made the move to another network.

It was the first program with no set format. Faced with this problem, Jerry Lester said, "What we have to do is change the idea of how we fill *time* to how we fill *tonight's time* and let tomorrow take care of itself."

"How do we do that?" asked someone.

"By acting like human beings and not performers," said Lester, setting the pattern for twenty years of late night shows to come.

It was an odds-against gamble and skeptical executives at the network stayed up late to catch the program. In addition to paying close attention to Dagmar's breathing exercises, they also wanted to see what late night television viewers would stay up to watch—or turn off. They wanted to see if a late night variety program could cut a hunk of the herd out of the late night movie stampede. And they wanted to find out if the affiliated stations were attracted to a show of that kind and if they would book it and split their income with NBC. Until then, local stations had been running old movies and keeping the money from the used-car dealer, the feed and grain store and the apple-corer pitchman who bought commercials during the breaks. What the network was playing with was a ready-made program to show on the stations which could receive it in those microwaveless, coaxial cableless days—in return for part of their income.

It was just one idea from Pat Weaver's dripping creative cornucopia.

Pat Weaver had more to do with the success of television than anything except the World Series and the coaxial cable. From the time he joined the National Broadcasting Company in 1949 until he was rudely ushered out of his job as Chairman of the Board in 1956, the tall, sandy-haired, jug-eared communications man gave the television medium depth, breadth, scope, intelligence, form, substance, revenue, professionalism and a lot of his own blood. Only the Bell Laboratory's transistor and the RCA color tube patents contributed as much to television's growth.

From Weaver's typewriter and his tape recorder and his dictated memos came the ideas, the forms, the outlines or the working theories for one-shot programs like *Peter Pan*, which was seen by over sixty-seven million people when it aired in 1954.

He managed to get over thirty million viewers to watch a classical ballet, *Sleeping Beauty*.

He created *Your Show of Shows* with Sid Caesar and Imogene Coca and changed America's Saturday movie nights into stay-home ones.

He gave the children *Howdy Doody* and *Ding Dong School* on NBC.

He developed the idea of rotating stars to keep them fresh and put on *The All Star Review* one night of the week and the *Colgate Comedy Hour* another.

He made sure that NBC carried *Zoo Parade* so that viewers could watch the fascinating lives of other animals and he developed *Wide, Wide World* so viewers could watch their own species at work and at play, at home and abroad.

And then he developed the *Today Show* to tell people what had happened during the night, the *Home Show* to help the American wife with her life, and the *Tonight Show* to relax and ease the viewer into bed and back to sleep where the *Today Show* could take over again.

During his seven years at NBC, Weaver came up with dozens of programs that he believed would turn mass man into class man.

One, *Operation Wisdom*, was set up to make a permanent recording of the world's greatest contributors. Starting in the early 1950s, Weaver camera crews shot long, talk-filled visits with philosopher Bertrand Russell, with poets Robert Frost and Carl Sandburg, with architect Frank Lloyd Wright. Weaver was heartbroken that educator John Dewey died before he could enshrine him.

Another Weaver thinkpiece was called *Operation Frontal Lobes* (because he had once read that the only difference between man and the animals was that man had frontal lobes in his brain). *Operation Frontal Lobes* was a series of documentaries ("telementaries" to Weaver) planned for prime-time exposure. (Prime time changes according to the network and the time of the year, but is usually that time when most people are watching the tube: most often somewhere between 6 and 10 P.M.)

The "telementaries" which Weaver wanted America's television watchers to take seriously were *The Birth Of A Baby*, *Western Mankind, The Atom, The Physical Universe* and even *The Grand Championships At A Dog Show.* He wanted to do shows on the glory that was Greece, on the White House, on the Monroe Doctrine, and on massive intellectual chunks of geographical, historical, psychological and political subjects he felt television owed its watchful audience.

Weaver was a different kind of president for NBC. Before he came in, there had been three men in the job in three years, all businessmen who were more concerned with balancing the books than with programming. Weaver was a professional communicator.

He was born on December 21, 1908, in Los Angeles. His father, Sylvester, Sr., was the head of a roofing materials company and before Junior reached his teens his father was a minor millionaire. His mother was a quiet woman who wrote poetry and played stringed instruments. In high school, the nicknamed "Pat" concentrated on dramatics and politics . . . two excellent backgrounds for survival in the network broadcasting industry.

Weaver went to Dartmouth where he specialized in philosophy and driving his Marmon at a rapid clip. He graduated in 1930 *magna cum laude*, then went to Europe to try writing while living on the Left Bank in Paris. The muse was out of town. Searching for her, he toured Egypt, Rome and the Mediterranean and then headed back to New York.

In tumbled profusion he had jobs selling a grocery store giveaway magazine, selling printing, and in the fall of 1932 he sold himself into a job at station KHJ, Los Angeles, as a writer-producer-salesman.

He moved to another radio job in San Francisco later and, not content with his growth there, moved to New York in 1935, where he cracked a job at NBC writing and producing one show and producing and hosting another one. He followed those jobs with his first important task, producing the Fred Allen *Town Hall Tonight* radio show, as a full-time employee of the Young & Rubicam advertising agency.

Weaver and Allen adopted each other immediately and Weaver stood at Allen's side, auditioning actors, making sure the program went on to Allen's liking, and heading off agents, clients and network brass who were trying to get through to Allen. He did it so well that within a couple of years Weaver was made head of all Young & Rubicam's radio programs.

One of the agency's clients was the American Tobacco Company and the head of the advertising department was George Washington Hill, Jr., son of the man who personally drove America crazy with slogans like "Reach for a Lucky Instead of a Sweet," "It's Toasted," and "Lucky Strike Green Has Gone to War! Yes, Lucky Strike Green Has Gone to War!" the commercial which explained a package color change as a national patriotic gesture. Hill, Jr., was taken with Weaver's ideas for advertising and for programming and talked his father into hiring Pat as the advertising manager.

Weaver added polish and programming savvy to American Tobacco's big programs, *Your Hit Parade, Kay Kyser and His College of Musical Knowledge* and *Information Please,* one of the early panel shows aimed at a mass audience.

During World War II, Weaver first served as a convoy duty

skipper in the South Atlantic and then was transferred to the Armed Forces Radio Service in Hollywood where he produced a show called *Command Performance.*

After the war he went back to the American Tobacco Company but when Hill, Sr., died, Weaver left there and returned to Y&R as head of their radio and television department and a member of the agency's executive committee, but he wanted more active participation in programming and less time in plans boards meetings. In 1949 he visited with Niles Trammell, then president of NBC, and also with Robert W. "Bobby" Sarnoff, who was then a close personal friend of his and the son of Brigadier General David Sarnoff, Chairman of the NBC board. Sarnoff arranged for Weaver to come to work as vice-president for television.

At the time he joined up with NBC, broadcasters were playing with television like a giant Erector set that had come with no assembly directions. Instead of being cowed by it, Weaver put it together in his own image.

He patented the word "communications." A newsroom became a communications center. The newscaster was a communicator. Weaver himself was the SuperCommunicator. Communications, when properly used, made Weaver predict that within fifty years the common man would become the uncommon man. He once said that television was more important to the history and development of mankind than the invention of printing type.

Weaver was a man with a mission and a sandwich board. He would show up at rubber chicken lunches, steak dinners or watermelon festivals to talk, talk, talk.

"I believe that man has come a long way fast," he said one day in 1955 to a group of advertising men in London, England, "and he can now make a quantum jump forward in a generation, largely due to television, for now we can see the day coming when a normal human being can handle the entire information load necessary to place himself in his own time with all the information about his history as a human being, as a member of a race, a nation, a creed, a faith, all the information about the universe he inhabits and its scientific description, all the information about the human culture he inherits and its achievements and its history; all the information about himself and the way he works as an individual; so that his personal balance and equilibrium can be stabilized; so that he can handle his life and growth intelligently; and all the information about his future and all futures projected so that he can select from among the myriad alternatives the kind of person he wants to become, the kind of a life he wants to lead, the kind of work he wants to do, the kind of achievements he can aim for."

In many ways, Weaver was also talking about his plans for the National Broadcasting Company.

One of the biggest changes Weaver brought to NBC and to network television itself was his "magazine" idea for underwriting the increasingly prohibitive costs of spectaculars, top stars and low-rated thinkpiece programs.

Until then, the advertising agencies had created and produced the programs and brought them to the networks for showing. All the network was selling then was the production facility and their time. It was like taking a bright child out to recite. The child remained the property of the parents even though the child recited in a school auditorium.

Under Weaver's "magazine" plan, the school owned the child and different sets of parents could "sponsor" a recital of "Mary-Had-A-Little-Lamb" or "Have-You-Seen-The Muffin-Man?"

Pat Weaver and NBC began to sell the complete, produced, on-air program instead of studio time and camera crews.

Weaver felt he had logic and reason and the smart network money on his side. Looking over the NBC line-up of television programs, he pointed out the confusion, conflicts and lack of continuity or common sense in the way shows were booked. There was no over-all master plan for scheduling.

Attempts to compete with the powerful CBS and the ambitious ABC networks for viewers was based upon the pulling power of individual programs or stars and not on time positions. Advertisers, through their agencies, were chunking in cheap shows that bought cheap audiences—quizzes, mysteries, audience participations and amateur hours.

In critical meetings, Weaver pointed out that, if television programming didn't improve, Americans weren't going to buy television sets. Ears perked up at NBC. That network was owned by the Radio Corporation of America and RCA held most of the highly profitable licenses and patents on television receiver components.

Weaver's attack against ad agency-orginated programming made sense to General Sarnoff and he gave Pat his blessings.

Weaver started to put together exciting, important shows. He hired the Jack Bennys, the Fred Allens, the Sid Caesars, the Max Liebmans, the Jerry Lewises. He opened NBC's purse and bought up expensive supporting casts, top writers and directors, symphony orchestras, spangled sets, lush costumes and the time to work with new camera techniques, new show ideas, new communications in his search to make television "not radio, not pictures, not vaudeville, but its own medium."

At the time, television was everybody else's. When it showed Arthur Godfrey it was radio with a camera turned on. When Skelton appeared it was his personal appearance act. Milton Berle was still a night club routine. *Philco Playhouse* was like a Broadway show. And Robert Montgomery was like a Hollywood movie.

The quiz shows, the amateur hours, the guess-that-tunes, the soap operas, even the news were all stale leftovers from radio but they were cheap and that was what ad agency clients wanted and that was what their agencies gave them.

Weaver's magazine format changed all of that. He dreamed up elaborate "magnet" shows which the network owned outright and then had his sales crew go out and offer pieces of them to the sponsors.

"It's really very simple," a salesman would explain. "It's just like buying a page in a magazine. The magazine gives you the stories and the articles and the cartoons and you buy a page or two pages in it. That way, you get credit for the whole magazine—or, in this case, the whole expensive show—without having to pay for all of it."

Revolutions are born hard.

On Madison Avenue, on Michigan Boulevard, on Wilshire, and especially at Young & Rubicam where Pat Weaver had once worked, the magazine concept was as welcome as the loss of a big client might be.

One Y&R executive who had worked with Weaver said, "Sure, when he was in agency programming, then he wanted us to do it. Now that he's at the network, he's on the other side. This plan does nothing for anybody except Pat."

His sidekick offered, "Look who's coming up with creative show ideas now—time salesmen and camera pushers. Hell, the good creative talent in the country is at the ad agencies, not at the networks."

One NBC salesman came back from a discouraging call and reported he was turned down this way. "NBC's Weaver is treading on holy ground. The American public, sir, associates the show with the product. . . . Fred Allen for Sal Hepatica, Jack Benny for Jell-O, Arthur Godfrey for Lipton's. For years we have been drilling that into their heads—that they get the entertainment as a reward for buying the product. We even end a couple of shows that way by saying, 'When you buy our pack we keep coming back.' Weaver wants to wipe all that out."

The final objection came from another agency: "How can we pick our audiences? Some of our clients want middle-aged housewives, some want young car buyers, some want the constipated crowd. Now we got shows going to each one. What's Weaver offer?"

For two years Weaver's special *Today-Home-Tonight* sales-men picked their way through those mine fields, offering single sponsorships here and there, yes, but pushing, pushing, pushing the magazine concept for two leftover minutes here and a minute there on the high-rated, talked-about programs like *Your Show of Shows* and *The All Star Revue*.

The breakthrough for Weaver's magazine concept was built into a program called *Today* which he dreamed up and put on in 1952. These were the days when network programming started at two in the afternoon. The idea of trying to sell the morning hours seemed as impossible as the idea of practical compatible color, back then.

One day Pat Weaver wandered into Mort Werner's office and asked, "What are the first things you think about when you wake up in the morning?"

Werner thought for a moment and then said, "That I have to go to the bathroom and what happened while I was asleep."

"Congratulations," said Weaver. "You've just become the producer of a show called *Today* and what happened while you were asleep is what it's all about."

Mort Werner had come to NBC through the jagged routes of bandleading, singing, managing a summer stock company, producing radio shows and managing radio stations. He had been recruited by NBC in 1951 to help develop television concepts and, between that year and 1955, Pat Weaver tagged him as executive producer for the *Today Show*, the *Home Show* and the *Tonight Show*. Werner is the man who was to hire Steve Allen, Jack Paar and Johnny Carson because "they are all exactly alike." Some NBC officials feel that the *Tonight Show* has much more Werner's touch than Weaver's influence around it, especially these days.

The first morning that the *Today Show* was to be presented, Werner got up at 3 A.M., dressed, and went outside his Scarsdale, New York, home to wait for the limousine ride into town.

An automobile slid over to the curb and Werner headed for it. It wasn't his ride but it was a Scarsdale police car.

"What're you doing out here, bud?" one of the patrolmen said, shining a flashlight in his face.

"I'm, uh, waiting for a ride into Manhattan. I'm, uh, a producer at NBC and I'm on my way to, uh, do a new show. It's called *Today*. Goes on at seven o'clock," Werner answered.

"Call the station and tell them we're bringing in a nut," the cop said to his partner. "Television shows at seven in the morning," he snorted.

Only when Werner's driver arrived and verified his story did the cops believe him. "Well, maybe you ain't nuts," one of them said as they were driving away, "but your network is —thinking anybody'll get up at that hour to watch television."

Two years later the formula was a success and Weaver said so. In one talk to the Baltimore Advertising Club, he said, "Every show developed by us [NBC] since 1949 as a pivotal hit has been developed as a multi-media sponsorship program. And this policy, adopted also by other networks, has been so successful that in 1953, NBC and CBS together had two hundred and sixty advertisers, one hundred and sixty-five for NBC and ninety-five for CBS. And here's a significant fact: In 1953, there were no less than eighteen advertisers on NBC who had less than $100,000 to spend on all media. Under the old pattern, they never could have afforded national exposure."

In short, Appian Way Pizza Mix could now sponsor the same program that General Motors did.

By the time that speech was made, Weaver had also launched the *Home* and *Tonight* shows because the *Today Show* had become a financial success. Working from a street-side studio in Manhattan, an easygoing slow-smiling Chicago personality named Dave Garroway held together a mixture of teletype news, recipes, weather reports, book and play reviews, local news, shopping tips, commuter timetables and interviews with celebrities, personalities, newsmakers and a chimpanzee.

The Executive Producer was Richard Pinkham, now the programming executive at the giant Ted Bates advertising agency in New York. The man in charge of getting advertisers for the shows was a sales genius named Matthew "Joe" Culligan. Pinkham remembers how they sold the *Today Show* to advertisers.

"We would go out, Joe and I, to the advertiser and his agency. Joe Culligan had been a magazine salesman so I listened to him. He got us a model of the *Today Show* set. There were different areas of the *Today Show* for different activities. A newsroom. A cooking room. An interview area. I showed the model and talked about how we were going to produce this new show. Then when I got finished, *he* asked for the order. We usually got it. We did the same thing before we put the *Home Show* on in 1953. As I remember, we had two million dollars in advertising before that show went on the air.

"When it came time to sell Pat Weaver's *Tonight Show*, Joe and I came up with another idea. The ad agencies weren't too enthusiastic about buying time late at night. From one place to another you'd get the same remarks. 'Everybody's sleeping or everybody's doing something else'—along with the snickers. But we got their attention with one simple device. I would stand up in front of them and read the television guide for that evening's late programming. Usually it was the fourteenth rerun of a black and white movie starring Mae Murray and Don Ameche and who wants to watch that? We made our point. They bought the *Tonight Show*."

Broadway Open House began to control late night television. Against the seventeenth rerun of *Plainclothes Man*, Dagmar and Company were getting nine out of ten homes that had TV sets turned on. In some cities, like Cleveland, the late night variety program was coming up with better ratings than NBC's biggest prime-time shows. But though the viewers were intrigued by the program, the local station managers weren't. They had a good thing going with local sponsors and inexpensive movies and they dragged their feet about cutting NBC in. After fifteen months the toldyouso's said, "I-told-you-so," and NBC decided to shut off America's nightly dose of foot-of-the-bed-lam.

One executive commented, "Pat didn't try too hard to save it. By the time it went off, he was up to his ass in new Weaverisms. He was going to make NBC into the American Communications Headquarters. He sent us plans for NBC to get into feature motion picture production, home-projectored movies, in-home kinescopes, Broadway shows, an opera touring company, microfilm newscasts you could punch up at home, real estate, phonevision, school communications equipment, fax machines that could transmit the whole of *Gone With the Wind* in seconds, control centers that could monitor any place in the world, even an NBC Guild for performers where they could get discounts and group medical plans and payments for replays of their kinescopes or films. Another of his nutty ideas."

Throughout his career, Weaver had often been accused of having "nutty" ideas. Some of this reputation came from his memos: long, rambling, involved pages filled with mixed academic references and abstract planning. He would quote the science of cybernetics for selling cigarettes. He employed the words of Albert Schweitzer to reach more housewives in Duluth. He encouraged his executives to leave the conventional, to think differently, to treat television not as radio with cameras or as motion pictures or plays but as its own medium and its own art form. They gathered after work in bar cars, whispered about his memos, tapped their heads significantly.

Once he came out with a program idea that had the NBC Symphony Orchestra seated at one end of a huge studio playing Josef Strauss's "Music of the Spheres" while Dr. Al-

bert Einstein sat at the opposite end of the studio staring
off into space and *thinking*.

Another time he planned a ninety-minute picture of autumn for the television audience. It was to be a symphony
played on a barge floating around Manhattan Island. He also
wanted to do a real Greek Play played by real Greeks in
a Greek theatre in either Los Angeles or Athens.

Many of his ideas worked out. Many were profitable. The
Today Show was. And when the *Tonight Show* finally went
on, it eventually earned its own way too:

Weaver continued to believe in the "fringe time" shows.
He pointed out the success of the *Today Show*: its audience
and the money it made. He continued to prod his programming executives to come up with a nighttime format that
could run the late movie shows off the air. They worked
on it. Finally Weaver okayed the project and the first *Tonight
Show* was under way.

Slated for September 27, 1954, the first news of the show
said it would be a combination of entertainment and service
features, that it was the logical extension of the *Today* and
Home Show magazine formats and that the show would also
have news and sports and weather inserts and anything else
any other NBC departments wanted to throw in.

"We couldn't decide whether to call it *Tonight* or *The
Waste Basket Revue*," one writer said.

The first news releases trumpeted, "At a time of night when
the Great White Way of Broadway is at its most glamorous,
the cameras of *Tonight* will bring the Crossroads of the
World to viewers across the country. There will be nu-
merous pickups from Times Square, center of Manhattan's
entertainment belt. Acting as 'Stagedoor Johnny' for millions
of viewers, *Tonight* will chat with the stars of Broadway's
biggest hits shortly after the curtains drop on evening performances. The important first nights of the theatre will
receive extensive *Tonight* coverage, with interviews with the
critics and other playgoers, stars and featured entertainers at

New York's smartest night clubs will be frequent visitors to the *Tonight* set."

Weaver stressed that the show would not be limited to New York, that mobile remote pickups would be carried from Chicago, from Hollywood, from Cleveland and New Orleans —wherever anything exciting was happening.

It was offered to all NBC stations as far west as Omaha, end of the transmission lines.

NBC described their new show host this way: "Steve Allen, who will star in *Tonight,* is one of the true native wits to spring into prominence in recent years, a man referred to by Groucho Marx as 'the best Allen since Fred.'" Steve Allen's qualifications took up one paragraph, Pinkham's two. Weaver's magazine concept and sales methods four.

From the beginning, the *Tonight Show* was a hit. Starting as a partially sustaining (money-losing) show, the program became self-supporting in ten months. Four months after that Pat Weaver was elected Chairman of the Board of the National Broadcasting Company and called a genius and a visionary and the greatest thing to happen to television since *Howdy Doody Time.*

One NBC executive, not quite so clap-hands about Weaver's rocketing career, was his friend and General Sarnoff's boy Robert. Weaver's star was so bright, it outshone the son, according to people who worked there.

One programming executive reports about that period, "Bobby went out of his way to make things tough for Pat. He knew that his growth in the company was limited as long as Pat was around, that Pat was the star, the hero, and that Pat held the job that Bobby wanted."

The young Sarnoff, according to reports, badgered, bothered and bugged Weaver. He used the name Sarnoff to get his way, pulled rank, ran to his father with stories and doubts about the efficiency and the wisdom of other executives, especially Weaver. The elder Sarnoff would call Weaver in for talks about the difficulties between the Chairman and his son. Weaver would often ask the General to get Bobby out of the network's hair but the General asked for patience.

One day, weary of it all, Weaver turned to another executive and said, "I just know when I die and get to heaven the good Lord is going to call me into his office and say, 'Listen, I've got a son I'd like you to work with. . . .'"

By 1956 the National Broadcasting Company was filled with snipers, spies, hatchetmen. There was a full-scale war on and either Pat Weaver or Robert Sarnoff would have to go. The elder Sarnoff fought for his son, put pressures on Weaver, and made new accomplishments almost impossible.

Robert W. Sarnoff was now President of NBC and he lost no time on September 7, 1956, getting out the news that Weaver had finally resigned and that the resignation had been accepted by the Board of Directors.

Most of the loyal Weaver men—the creators of *Today* and *Tonight* and *Wide, Wide World* and *Victory at Sea* and hundreds of other milestones in television's golden years— were immediately fired. New ones loyal to Robert W. were moved up or hired.

Almost before Weaver had taken his last down elevator at 30 Rockefeller Plaza, people were in his offices packing up books, throwing out memos, tossing pictures of the kids, pens, awards, calendars and a coffee cup into empty boxes.

Going through the papers, one junior executive noticed a 1953 memo that said, "You know who will be the first men on the moon. . . . You will. Every man here can be there because it will be a television carrying . . . aircraft that makes the flight."

"What a wacko he was," said the junior exec, shaking his head and packing up what was to go.

What was to stay were the only truly original television concepts ever developed. . . .

3

The *Tonight Show* was supposed to follow the *Today Show*.

It was to be relaxed, casual, easygoing.

It was to have comedy, music, reviews, interviews and a continuing cast.

It was to be cheap to produce.

And expensive to buy.

And it was to make money for NBC.

As the *Today Show* had done.

Today had not always been successful. NBC's master salesman, Joe Culligan (who once described himself as an honest confidence man), and producer Richard Pinkham had had a tough time selling the advertising agencies on a radio-wakeup-show-with-pictures. Advertisers weren't convinced that people would turn on television sets at seven in the morning and, even if they did, they were certainly in no mood to buy anything except maybe orange juice, coffee or a Bromo. But what do ad agencies know? NBC Vice-President Pat Weaver told NBC Executive Producer Dick Pinkham to go ahead. Pinkham told NBC Producer Mort Werner to get it produced. And at 7 A.M. on January 14, 1952, during the reign of Harry the Truman, the first telecast of the *Today Show* went out to twenty-six stations in the NBC network.

Although only two hours of the show were seen in any one city, the show was actually telecast for three hours each day because of the time difference between New York and Chicago.

There was exactly *one* paid commercial on that first telecast and there were later days during that early period when there were exactly *no* words from the sponsor.

Within eight months the show was a spectacular flop and was losing over a million and a half dollars for the network. The toldyouso's continued to laugh at NBC in newspaper columns, in ad agency media departments, in advertising managers' offices. At NBC, the ambitious young executives who sided with Weaver and Werner were suddenly seen visiting with Robert Sarnoff's aides or dictating "I-had-nothing-to-do-with-the-*Today-Show*" memos to whoever would read them.

But, yawningly, sleepily, surely but slowly, people began snapping on the *Today Show* as a morning habit. One family cut a hole in the kitchen wall so they could watch the living-room TV set from the breakfast table. Others bought automatic timers and clock radios and hooked their sets up so that the *Today Show* started their Todays. One lady had a television set mounted on the wall of her bedroom so she could watch without getting up. A man wrote to the program and asked if they would do something backward because he always watched it in his bathroom mirror while shaving.

The production crew of the show tried everything to get viewers to turn it on. They tried beauty queens, prime ministers, baseball players, horn blowers, authors, cabinet members, hypnotists, prognosticators and fashion shows. And while they kept trying in the studio, Joe Culligan kept trying outside.

"It's a relaxed, low-pressure, member-of-the-family kind of program," Culligan would tell one advertiser. "When everybody in the family is grumpy and sleepy, it's nice to have a pleasant voice around the house," he would tell an advertising manager. "It's something to look at instead of an unshaven husband or a curler-headed wife," he would tell the ad agency vice-presidents.

It began to work.

In 1953 sponsors began to buy a spot here and a commercial there sometime between 7 and 9 A.M. and by late 1954 the *Today Show* was being seen by two and a half million viewers in forty-nine cities. To top that, the show had a gross income of over eleven million dollars and that amount set a new one-year income record for the entire spectrum of show business including radio, circuses and vaudeville.

More importantly, the *Today Show* had created the feeling, the mood, the attitude of magazine format shows including the to-be-born *Home, Tonight,* Cavett, Frost, Bishop, Griffin presentations and even the smaller-audienced talk shows like Dinah Shore, Virginia Graham and A.M.

The man who created that mood was a lank-haired, honeytoned disc jockey from Chicago named Dave Garroway. Even the most sourly awakened couldn't get mad at him, couldn't throw even a slipper at the TV set. Garroway talked softly, chuckled a lot, moved slowly, slouched against studio furniture, mused away dreamily for minutes at a time, wandered casually through commercials, often changing them as he went along, and held up his hand, palm out, and said, "Peace": the first television personality to use that phrase— besides the clergy on Sunday mornings.

Pat Weaver's concept called for Garroway to be a "master communicator." NBC surrounded him with tapping teletypes, flashing red lights, buzzers, many time-zone-telling clocks on the wall, facsimile machines, meteorological charts, rear motion picture projectors, front motion picture projectors, slide projectors, ringing telephones, TelePrompTers, the newest cameras on silent-glide pedestals, miniaturized microphones, high-intensity lighting, a first-rate crew, a studio located in a show window right on the street, and even small boys with rolled-up sleeves who ran around the set, sheafs of still-wet newspapers ruffling in their hands.

Through it all, Garroway ambled aimlessly and, suddenly finding something or someone of interest, would look up surprised at a camera and murmur, "Say, Old Tigers, look what I've got here."

What he had "got there" could be anything from J. Fred Muggs, the resident chimpanzee, to a standing dissertation on the importance of the human thumb, to the President of the United States.

In the days when the show had not been going too well, somebody came up with the idea of using a chimp to give early morning grouches a good laugh. Although J. Fred Muggs behaved fairly well on camera, he could be a major problem before, after and sometimes during the show. He often urinated on the sets, on the desks, on the crew, on the guests and on his costumes. When he wasn't doing that, he was biting somebody or something. The somebody could be Garroway, who more than once had to hide his bleeding hand from the camera and smile through his tears. The something he bit ranged from camera cables to a diamond ring worn by Lee Meriwether, Miss America. Meriwether worked on the show back then (there were twenty-nine different female assistants-commentators-interviewers or combinations thereof before the current lady, Barbara Walters, nailed down the job in a fairly secure manner) and one day Muggs pulled a large diamond ring from her finger and promptly popped it into his mouth. It took half the crew to get his mouth open and to recover the ring.

"I guess the engagement's over," somebody said to Lee later.

As for thumbs, Garroway was leaning back in his chair twiddling them one day when he suddenly came up with one of his morning musings. Holding one up to a nearby lighted camera, he shook his head at the wonder of it all and said, "Without this happy little digit, what would our babies suck on?" he asked. "Just imagine sticking a stamp with a fist, or hitching a ride with a third finger, right hand. Let's face it, Old Tigers, without this useful item, we'd still be crawling around in the caves." At 7 A.M. the thumb was as good a subject as any, to Garroway.

Another day, during one of his rambles, Garroway looked casually out one of the large show windows which made up one wall of his 49th Street studio. One of the faces pushed against the window, watching the show, was the President of the United States, Harry S Truman. One of the directors spotted him and had a camera wheeled toward the window. The President moved on when he saw the camera but paused at the next window for a moment. By then, a member of the production crew had run out into the street and asked Truman to come in and visit.

"He can't," said his companion, who turned out to be comedian George Jessel. "He's too busy. Besides," added Jessel, pulling himself up, "I work for another network."

From that time to now, just about everybody but the President has been *on* the *Today Show*. From the first guest, Fleur Cowles, a magazine editor who put out a flossy diecut publication called *Flair*, until now, the *Today Show* has paraded before its six to seven million daily viewers a never ending string of authors, naturalists, fashion designers, home-run hitters, archaeologists, jewelers, ingenues, politicians, party givers, big tippers, self-improvers, God-seekers, sex sellers and people with quaint, charming, funny or frightening hobbies, items or attitudes.

Many uninvited people, like the President, made appearances on the show by elbowing their way into the first row outside the huge NBC Exhibition Hall windows and making faces or signs to show the folks at home.

Most of them pushed causes like banning the bomb or lowering the subway fare or getting the U.N. out of the U.S. One time an out-of-towner held up a crudely lettered placard that said, "Look, Maw, no hangover." Another time a man raised a sign that said, "WATCH HERB SHELDON ON TV RIGHT NOW—CHANNEL 7." Herb Sheldon was a performer who had an early morning program at the same time on another network. For a while there was a spate of personal messages like "MARSHA CALL ME JOHN" and "BILLY COME BACK WE LOVE YOU" and of course, the inevitable "JESUS SAVES" and the "EAT AT JOE'S" and the "SPECIAL SALE AT KLEIN'S" but the cameras cut rapidly away from the commercial or the offensive.

During his years at NBC, one group of co-workers felt that Garroway was a delightful, low-pressure, easygoing type. Another group believed him to be "pixilated" or touched by the elves.

One network executive who was assigned to the show still tells the story of an alleged meeting with Garroway in the NBC executive washroom. The storyteller was washing his hands at the basin when he heard somebody calling from behind the closed door of one of the stalls.

"Hey, come here, will you? Look at this," the voice asked.

The NBC man approached warily and said, "Huh?"

"Come here, come here a minute, I want to show you something."

"What? What's that?" the man answered, approaching more closely.

"Look at this," said Garroway, opening the door suddenly. He was seated on the plumbing, his right hand pointing down to the trousers and underwear around his ankles.

"Look at what?"

"Right there, can't you see it? They've done it again."

"Done what? Who's done what?"

"Can't you see it? My underwear's on backwards. The poltergeists have turned my underwear around again."

"Turned it around, eh? Again, eh?"

"Sure. I put it on right in the morning and, you know, three or four times a day when they get pesky, they turn my underwear around."

"Say, that's a problem," said the network man, edging toward the washroom door. "You should do something about it."

"Going to," said Garroway. "Going to have a stern talk with them about doing that."

If, as that man and others believe, Garroway was truly touched by poltergeists, it could easily be because he was born on the thirteenth of July in 1913 at 13 Van Valson Street in the 13th Ward of Schenectady, New York.

His father, David Cunningham Garroway, was a soft-spoken engineer who worked for the General Electric Company. His mother seldom raised her voice. One time, Garroway remembers, the family had bought a baby grand piano. Curious about its workings, young Garroway removed the hammers and keys from the sounding board. The only scolding he received was a firm suggestion that he reconstruct the instrument. The quiet home environment plus the insecurity of changing schools twenty-one times during his childhood gave Garroway his soft-spoken, approach-it-slowly attitudes toward life.

After graduation from Washington University in St. Louis, it didn't seem to make much difference what he did. He first tried astronomy and was hired as the man who unlocked the door and pulled back the shutter on the telescope at the Harvard Observatory. After that he tried selling piston rings, then switched to selling a textbook on pronunciation to schoolteachers. The book contained 800 of the most hard-to-pronounce words in the English language. To sell the book, Garroway asked prospective customers to pick out any five words. If the customer pronounced them correctly, Garroway would give them the book. But if one or more were pronounced wrong, the prospect was to purchase it. It was during this period that Garroway picked up the many multisyllabic phrases he used later on television.

His first job in broadcasting was as a fifteen-dollar-a-week pageboy at NBC. Interested in radio, he spent the time he wasn't steering audiences into seats attending announcing school. He graduated twenty-third in a class of twenty-four. By asking around, however, he landed a job at station KDKA in Pittsburgh as a special sports announcer. He broadcast golf matches from a portable transmitter hung on his back while he was entered in them. He once broadcast a canoe race and ended it with a gurgle. He swam with a water polo team and described the action splash by splash. He described what it feels like to be a bowling ball going down an alley to make a strike. He also broadcast from a bridge under construction, from a submarine in the Ohio River and even from a piece of steel that was being riveted into a new high-rise building.

When World War II came along, Garroway went into the U. S. Navy as an ensign and while on duty in Honolulu started an after-hours disc jockey show at station KGU. One night, while searching for a record, he began talking about Chicago. He rambled along, mentioning the people, the places, the sights of the Windy City, just chatting, talking, mumbling along. Before he had the next record on, the telephone calls were coming in from homesick Chicago servicemen and from other G.I.s and sailors who wanted Garroway to talk about their home towns too. It was at that point Garroway realized he had developed a definite style that he called "Old Buddy."

After the war he continued to perfect that style on a midnight till 2 A.M. disc jockey show which went to, as he said, "short-order cooks and burglars." Later, he added daytime shows. Listening to one of them was a man named Jules Herbuveaux, manager of station WNBQ in Chicago. He was enchanted with the soft, easy sell of Garroway's approach. In 1948 a writer named Charley Andrews, and Ted Mills, the chief of production, talked to Herbuveaux about a television show called *Garroway at Large* which would be an extension of Dave's easygoing radio shows. Given the okay, they hired singers Jack Haskell, Connie Russell and Betty Chapel and comedian Cliff Norton. The program was about to go on the air in Chicago when New York called and asked what they had for a Sunday night spot on the network. Suddenly, *Garroway at Large* was on the coaxial cable and in the living rooms and hearts of millions of his countrymen.

At the time, television had few restrictions or rules. Directors, cameramen, writers and performers like Garroway all worked to come up with the unusual, the strange, the exotic, the welcome change—to explore the potentials of this new medium.

Some of the new tricks became sight gags. One time Garroway signed off by saying, "This show originated in Chicago, the short end of the coaxial cable." He bent down, picked up a cable and disappeared in a cloud of smoke, to the music of his theme song, "Sentimental Journey."

On one show they painted a large bed linen to hold up at show's end. It said, "This sheet came to you from Chicago."

Another time Garroway talked about how Chicago wasn't like Hollywood. In Chicago you could trust your friends. He turned to walk away from the camera and viewers saw a large knife sticking out of his back.

They worked on and perfected many new camera techniques. In one they matched a man playing a harmonica with a man eating an ear of corn. They held a ribbed glass brick in front of the camera and got sixty-four images of Connie Russell singing a song. They used the "subjective camera" device which treats the lens of the camera as the viewer's eye. They had a dentist's drill seem to grind the lens. They emptied drinks into the picture. They used mirrors and unusual camera locations to shoot up, down and inside skits, performances and acts.

The sponsor for all of this was a flooring company and Garroway handled their commercials with the same nonchalance he used during the rest of the show. He made the sales pitch so relaxed and so warm that long-time television observers say it was the first case of the audience liking the commercials as well as the programming.

All over the country, sponsors and advertising agencies were taking a second look at Garroway and his "Chicago school" of television. The word "intimacy" was suddenly used by network brass to explain Garroway's appeal to the television audience.

"On one hand you have the coarse, rude shouting of a Milton Berle, and on the other you have the warm intimacy of Garroway," they said, proving they could use the word in a sentence. Suddenly, it was smart to call television an intimate medium.

During the summer of 1951 several sponsors bid for the *Garroway at Large* program and one signed up for it. Assured of working the following autumn, Garroway and program writer Charley Andrews headed for Europe to take a stretched-out vacation. They were in the Swiss Alps when an early morning telegram arrived from New York.

Garroway opened it, read it, shook Andrews awake. He said something like, "Get up and look at the most beautiful sunrise in the world." Then he added, "And also, we're out of work." The network had decided not to carry *Garroway at Large* any more, for scheduling reasons.

They headed back for New York and, once there, Garroway heard that Pat Weaver was looking for a "communicator" to host the new NBC *Today Show.* Garroway got to Mort Werner, who listened interestedly, then got him to Pat Weaver, who was quite aware of Garroway's mumbling style, visual humor and the soft-sell-hard-sell success of his commercials.

Weaver gave his blessings.

"Old Tiger," said Garroway to himself, "you're now a communicator, go communicate."

Garroway's *Today Show* looked easy, relaxed, informal. He read the news, joked with announcer Jack Lescoulie, read the weather reports, showed a short film or two on a topical subject, reviewed a book, talked about a new movie, had J. Fred Muggs play the piano, visited with a guest like a cab driver who told how to get a cab in the rain and, in general, filled 180 minutes with a continuous flow of bright, interesting, sometimes funny talk, talk, talk.

Communications on the show were so casual that directions for the crew were often left around in hastily scribbled memos.

One note left for the get-ready crew said: "7:25—Cleveland Armory."

The crew man assigned to arrange things read it, scratched his head, read it again, then picked up the telephone and called NBC, Cleveland.

He told the Cleveland end that at seven twenty-five in the morning New York would be all set for the feature from Cleveland and wanted to know if Cleveland was all ready. Cleveland, not to be flustered either, said they would call right back. Cleveland got on the local phone, rousted the armory caretaker out of bed and had him go downtown and unlock the place.

At the appointed time, the Cleveland Armory was open, the NBC employee in Cleveland smiling, the armory caretaker smiling, the *Today Show* man smiling.

"Cleveland Armory's ready," he reported to the director.

"Where is he?" the director asked.

"He? What He?"

"Cleveland Amory, the author, the guest for the show this morning. You said he's ready. Where?"

When the show began making money and getting ratings

and went over seven million viewers, Pat Weaver said that was the kind of show he wanted to put on late at night too. The *Broadway Open House* format had been all wrong, he pointed out. Too frantic, too much bustle, too much burley-cue house slapstick and fraternity house horseplay and cat-house sex.

"Let's see if we can't open up the network nighttime fringe hours with a relaxed, warm show people will watch and sponsors will buy," he said to the people who worked for him.

"Just as soon as we find the right guy to run it," they assured him.

☆ **4**

"The qualities of a good physician are these," said the radio announcer rattling off the drugstore commercial, ". . . the heart of a lion, the eye of an eagle, the hand of a woman . . . the yolk of an egg, two cups of flour and three tablespoons of brown sugar."

From the sea-warped fishing shacks in Ventura County to the beer-polished bars of Los Angeles County to the Quonset-hut American Legion halls in Orange County, hundreds of thousands of radio listeners gasped, chortled, smiled, snickered, bellowed, whooped, sniggered, chuckled at their favorite funnyman: a disc jockey who looked like an owl but acted like a cuckoo.

The year was 1950. The human record player was a man named Stephen Valentine Patrick William Allen. The time was midnight. The station was KNX, the CBS outlet in Los

Angeles. The format and formula that would become the television *Tonight Show* four years later were being born.

And so were the style and the manner and the snappy patter of the performer who would bring the *Tonight* television program to the air and give it what some people say were its only golden years.

Back then, back in 1950, people listened to radio, especially in Los Angeles. Even today, the city of the angels has more radio listeners than any city in the United States. Los Angeles also has more "out of home" radios, more car radios, more portable, more boat, more pedestrian radios than most cities have total listeners. Advertisers spend as much on radio in Southern California as they do on television in most other sections of the country. Southern Californians spend a lot of time away from their television sets but near a radio. That's why in-car FM radio, in-car stereo and in-car cassette recordings are all California-popularized customs. Between the boat radio, the car radio and the portable (one department store ran a "Stick It In Your Ear" sale for portable radios), the Southern Californian is and always has been equipped with an ear on one side of his head and a superheterodyne receiver on the other.

This, then, makes the local disc jockey more than a man who reads commercials, puts records on a turntable and tells Sheila that Mike dedicates this record to her and to the boys down at the Honda garage. Radio personalities in Los Angeles can and do make hundreds of thousands of annual dollars, can hold steady jobs (one has been on the same station for more than twenty years) and can become super-celebrities—the kind celebrities tune in. In a town where nearly everyone knows the mothers of, the hairdressers of, or the high-colonic administers of, movie stars and television personalities, the disc jockey remains a god. He opens supermarkets, leads off at Pro-Am golf tournaments, endorses politicians, hosts award dinners, breaks ground, opens nights, and always sits on the fifty-yard line. A Southern California

disc jockey can make or break a dance, a city councilman, a recording, a charity, morning traffic and a radio station worth
millions of dollars.

Of all of this and all of these, Steve Allen was considered
the jauntiest and the jolliest of the jocks. For his late night
radio program, college students stopped studying, sleepers
rose to catch him, firemen prayed for no alarms while he
was on, gag writers took pen and carbon paper in hand,
and starlets voted him the man they "went to bed with"
most often.

Listeners knew what they were going to hear when they
listened to Steve Allen. They would hear good jazz records
and some short lectures on jazz. They would hear screen or
night club personalities who came in to visit, perform or
plug their next act, feature or booking. They would hear
commercials, more or more likely less as the advertising agency
had written them. And they would hear comments like
these:

Guest: Steve, do they get this show in Pasadena?
Allen: They hear it but they don't get it.

Or

"That short message from the sponsor is now available
on long-playing records."

Or

"What do you do with that shovel?"
"I dig."
"I'm hip."

Steve Allen had originally been hired in 1948 to run an
eleven-thirty-to-midnight, five-night-a-week straight record
show. For two years before this, Allen and a partner named
Wendell Noble had starred in a morning comedy show on the
Mutual network. Short of budget and afraid to tell the
network they were running out of material after their initial
success, Noble and Allen had crammed some five hundred
shows full of material from old joke books, high school dog-

gerel, sound-effect gimmicks, parodies, comedy voices, satires on soap operas, college magazine jokes, and created characters: a Mexican named Manuel Labor, a hunter named Claude Horribly.

A young organist who had just been discharged from the Air Corps became their accompanist. His name was Skitch Henderson and he later became the band leader on Allen's *Tonight Show*.

When Allen took over the late night record show, he felt that he knew every old joke ever written or knew how to write jokes on any subject. He could also milk a joke longer than a used-car commercial.

Allen wasn't highly enthused about the record show. He wanted a program that would be more of a showcase but he needed the money and the job at KNX was the only speaking part in town.

The station management wanted it simple. "Play the records," they said, "and in between just a few comments. We don't want exactly a straight announcer or a disc jockey. Somebody sort of in between."

That was the only invitation Steve Allen needed to start turning that late radio hour into a stage for Steve Allen instead of a platform for Bing Crosby, Frankie Laine and Dinah Shore. From the first program on he made himself more important than the records.

For the first two months he would play a record, talk for a couple of minutes, play another record, talk some more. He dragged out old jokes, new puns, offbeat sayings and ideas. California's radio listeners began to listen to Allen, to write him notes, to call him.

One day the KNX programming department sent a memo. "Listen, Steve," it said, "this is supposed to be a record show, not a talk show. When we want a comedy show we'll ask for one."

Allen asked his listeners for help. He read the executive memo on the air that night. Within the next two days, more than four hundred letters came in telling KNX to let Allen do his show his way.

Allen used those letters to convince KNX management that Los Angeles was ready for a light talk show at a late night hour.

CBS executives compromised with him, asked him to play a record now and then.

The format for the to-be *Tonight Show* was a-borning.

Allen then introduced the studio audience; another comedy device that would be used in the television *Tonight Show*.

Initially, there had been no audience for the record show. Allen had broadcast from a small studio with a desk, a microphone and three chairs in it. As he became more popular, friends of his—musicians, other comedians, actors and writers—would drop by to see him. Sometimes they laughed right out loud on the air when Steve got off a good remark. Listening at home, people heard the laughter and assumed there was a studio audience. Soon, requests for tickets began to come in and the station management realized that the show was catching on. They moved Steve to a larger studio, one that could seat about fifty, and they doubled the time of his show to fifty-five minutes. His salary, however, stayed at a hundred dollars a week.

Shortly after he had moved into the new studio, the KNX management saw that the show was completely out of hand. More than a hundred people a night were showing up to sit in the fifty seats from eleven until midnight.

One person who did not show up one particular night was Doris Day. She had been scheduled to guest on the program by her publicity agent but nobody had bothered to tell Doris about it. Since being on Steve's program had turned into a sign of importance, and since scheduled guests had always shown up before this, Allen was unprepared for a hole in his show. It was suddenly eleven-thirty that particular night. He had run through his twenty-five minutes of prepared material and was on the verge of doing thirty minutes of "Silent Night."

Desperate for anything, Allen decided to try the audience for laughs. He picked up the heavy, floor-stand microphone and walked into the audience with it. From the first question to the first audience member, Allen knew he had a new kind of comedy—people off guard, offhand and sometimes off base. Radio personality Art Linkletter, of course, and Tom Brenneman of *Breakfast in Hollywood* had been doing it for years but their interviews had devices in them like, "Which lady has been married longest?" or "Who has a recipe for real German sauerbraten this morning?" Allen's approach started from the innocent comment made by the person being interviewed and then ended with a clever comment, a gag, a joke, a punch line or, sometimes, a complete routine. They went something like this:

Guest: Hey, can they hear me at home in Wheeling?
Allen: I don't know. Do they have an appointment?
Guest: I said I'd say hello to them.
Allen: When did you see them last?
Guest: This morning.
Allen: You traveled three thousand miles to California to say hello to somebody you saw this morning?

The audience would howl, punch one another in the ribs, hold their sides and try to stop tears from streaming down their faces.

From the first time he tried it, working with the audience became a nightly routine and the highlight of the program. Allen's ratings shot up. Young movie stars stayed up to hear his "hip" humor and so did Ethel Barrymore, Fanny Brice and Al Jolson, who called the program "the best show on the air." One night after *The Jolson Story* film had been released, the jazz singer came on the Allen program and did an entire hour of songs and little-known autobiographical material.

Another night Allen went head to head with jokes and ad libs with a little-known New York comedian named Jackie Gleason. The next morning ex-movie star and then film director Ida Lupino sent word out that she wanted the "funny one" for a new film. Only when Steve showed up ready for his big break in Hollywood did somebody tell him that Lupino had wanted Gleason and not Allen.

During this period the CBS people also gave Allen an early evening radio program to do. It was a more structured type of comedy show and to help him with his busy schedule the programming people gave him two staff writers: Bob Carroll, Jr., and a very small girl with a very large sense of humor named Madelyn Pugh. Later, the two of them were to create some of the characterizations and outstanding comedy of *The Lucy Show* for many years.

Soon the Allen show just about controlled Southern California radio between eleven and midnight. At times the studio audience ran over a thousand people and some of them would stand in line for four or five hours to get a front-row seat. Allen noticed that the people who waited were usually the most aggressive ones in the audience, the ones who could toss him unintentionally funny lines. He would have people on the show or ushers watch for the "kooks" or characters in the audience, so he could pick out one or two of them to "work" during the interview parts of the show.

He also learned early not to fight with his guests. He found that comedians didn't want to come on the show because it was "Allen's House" and that he enjoyed the home-team advantage. Allen adopted a philosophy of leaving comedians alone, of letting them do their material without interruption, without ad libs from him, and without fear of being topped. Allen practiced being the straight man for comedians, for one-syllable starlets, for beginning performers. He continued this practice on his later *Tonight Show* and Johnny Carson usually follows those rules today. Of the

Tonight Show hosts, only Jack Paar continually tried to top his guests and to make himself funny by poking fun at other people's appearances or performances.

One night when singer Frankie Laine was on the show, Allen complained that the amateur song writer didn't have a chance. Although there were about four million people in the country who were capable of writing songs, Allen said, only about four hundred songs a year really sold. The toughest part of song writing, Allen continued, wasn't the writing but getting them published. Allen pressed on, insisting he could write three hundred and fifty songs a week and that writing them was no trick at all.

Laine disagreed with him and they made an on-air bet of a thousand dollars that Allen couldn't compose fifty songs a day for seven days. Allen not only won the bet but (a) he did it in the show window of Hollywood's largest music store and (b) composed most of them within an hour each day by turning on a tape recorder and just ad-libbing them until he had reached fifty. He later admitted that some of the three hundred and fifty melodies had bridges or front strains or melody lines that were similar or even identical to other published songs but the duplication had been subconscious and not deliberate at all. Even deducting the few imitations, Allen had easily turned out over three hundred melodies in a week. It is still the production record for music men.

Today, Allen is one of this country's most prolific writers of songs. Since the radio period in 1949 and 1950 when he began to compose music, he has turned out close to three thousand songs including "An Old Piano Plays the Blues," which was recorded by Nat "King" Cole and Hoagy Carmichael, and "Let's Go to Church Next Sunday Morning," which was one of the tunes he ground out during his week-in-the-window. It was recorded by Western singing star Jimmy Wakely and by Margaret Whiting and by Perry Como. He also did the lyrics for "South Rampart Street Parade," which Bing Crosby and the Andrews sisters recorded. He wrote "Impossible," "Pretend You Don't See Her," "The Gravy Waltz" and "This Could Be the Start of Something" which became his theme song and which, today, has recordings made of it by Tony Bennett, Jack Jones, Steve Lawrence and Eydie Gorme, Dorothy Collins, Les Brown, June Valli and more than ninety other artists, groups and bands.

All of this time Steve Allen had Southern Californians falling off of drive-in stools, off of automobile bucket seats, off of custom round beds with laughter, his agent, Jules Green, was working hard to get him out of a local station and onto the CBS network.

"Steve's a star!" he would shout into the telephone. "How can you stand in his way?"

At the other end of the line in New York was a CBS network programming executive named Hubbell Robinson. At the time, CBS had holes in its programming, programs that were slipping, and a static star list. Robinson listened carefully, talked with California CBS programming people, looked at his line-up, shrugged and indicated that CBS would do its best to make a place for Steve Allen.

And in November of 1950 the man *Variety* trade paper called "that ad-glibber Steve Allen" moved to CBS, New York. Robinson wanted Allen in New York because the shows he had in mind for him originated there. At the time there was no coaxial cable. Programs done in New York were seen up to two weeks later in California by way of delayed kinescopes or films taken off the tube.

Allen had a mental picture of New York audiences and it spooked him. "I had read theatre reviews for years and other performers had told me how tough and sophisticated New York audiences were. I expected a whole theatre full of people who looked, dressed and acted like Noel Coward. I was really surprised and very relieved to find that my audiences were made up of old ladies whose feet hurt and college kids who laughed at anything."

For a while Allen had a good look at different audiences and audiences had a good look at a different kind of personality.

One of the first times CBS officials realized that Steve Allen was not your basic number 24 host happened a few days after he arrived in New York.

Arthur Godfrey's plane was in Florida and so was Arthur and so was bad weather. A CBS executive asked Allen to sit in for Godfrey on that night's *Talent Scouts* program.

Allen still believes that he made a shambles of the program. The audience believes he made it a memorable experience. He opened the show in pure Allen style.

"This is Arthur Godfrey," he said, strolling onto the stage. "Well, this isn't Arthur Godfrey really, I was just trying to scare my wife."

The waves of laughter washed people out of their seats.

From there on, and Allen says non-intentionally, he brought total calamity to the program. He continually forgot the contestants' names, made a cup of hot Lipton's tea with a package of soup mix, poured the soup into Godfrey's ukulele, and announced all the wrong people as winners on the show. The ad agency fellows didn't think Allen was very funny but Godfrey did. He had been tuned in and he called Allen to congratulate him on a very funny show.

CBS tried Allen at left field, at short stop and as a relief runner. They tried him as a quiz master on a summer replacement show for *Our Miss Brooks*. When that went off, they put him in as host and emcee of *Songs for Sale*, a program that showcased musical numbers by amateur writers. By July 30, 1951, he had his own program—the *Steve Allen Show*—which was on CBS network at noon five days a week. And he was doing the *Songs for Sale* program on Saturday nights. He was putting in eight and a half public hours a week, most of them on camera reading his mail, eating foods sent in by adoring fans, talking to the audience, playing the piano, acting out sight gags, interviewing guest performers and, in short, working out more of the format he was to take to the original *Tonight Show.*

Time magazine gave him a four-paragraph review that summer; ". . . he is getting a lot of laughs, good reviews, $2000 a week for playing one of the simplest (and most difficult) of roles: that of the natural, nice guy who occasionally comes out with a funny crack."

In 1953, Allen's relationship with CBS suddenly thinned. *Songs for Sale* had been on for a year and a half and when it went off for the summer hiatus in 1953, Allen assumed that it would be back in the fall. However, CBS programming executives had been taken by a comedian named Jackie Gleason who was working on an independent channel in New York. They decided to build a show around Gleason and put that show in the time slot reserved for *Songs for Sale.* There were no other openings during evening prime time so the executives asked Steve if he would do the show in the afternoons instead. Allen refused.

Part of the reason he turned it down was a general unhappiness with CBS. It had been only a short time before that the network had canceled his daytime noon show because it "just wasn't making it."

By that time Steve was down to his last radio show—a half-hour format which CBS told him would be a showcase for the "old, natural Allen." Allen responded, "What was that Allen the last year and a half?" He became a panelist on the popular television game show, *What's My Line?* He joined newspaper columnist Dorothy Kilgallen, television personality Arlene Francis, publisher Bennett Cerf and the show's host, John Daly.

Thinking about it today, Allen remembers only that he usually didn't recognize the mystery guest even with the mask off and that he created the immortal question, "Is it bigger than a breadbox?" He never understood why that line of all lines asked by all panelists for all those years should be the best remembered.

When Jerry Lester's *Broadway Open House* went off the air in late summer of 1951, NBC gave the late hours back to their affiliated stations and went out of network-run late night television programming. However, in New York the ABC station was telecasting a late night variety program conducted by a comedian named Louis Nye. Later, Nye was to become part of Allen's men-on-the-street along with Don Knotts, Tom Poston, Bill Dana, Dayton Allen and Don Adams. Nye's greatest claim to fame was his parody of a New York ad man who started his on-camera interviews with "Hi-ho, Steverino."

The program on ABC was sponsored by the local Ruppert Brewery. Its most loyal viewer was a man named Ted Cott. Cott was head of WNBT, the NBC-owned-and-operated station in Manhattan. Cott wanted the beer business. He decided that he could do the late night show better than ABC was doing it. He said so to the beer company and he offered them Steve Allen as the master of ceremonies.

Steve Allen's agent, Jules Green, had been one of the first people to get Cott's attention. When Allen's shows at CBS began to disintegrate, Green went to NBC and asked if they would make a kinescope of a five-night-a-week ("strip") show if he, Green, would go out and sell it. Cott said that he had an idea for the perfect program. "Sort of a Tonight's Show." It would be sponsored by Knickerbocker Beer and it would be on the air from 11:20 P.M. (later from eleven) until midnight.

Steve Allen knew the format he wanted. Cott had the money and the time. From July 27, 1953, the *Tonight Show* idea was to begin an uninterrupted (although often reformulated and repopulated) run that is now into its twentieth year.

NBC gave Allen the studio that was used by the Skitch Henderson and Faye Emerson, and the Tex and Jinx daytime shows. Cott assigned a producer named Johnny Sterns to the program and a youngish, ex-camera-dolly pusher named Dwight Hemion to direct it. Hemion, today, is recognized as the best director of television musical and variety programs. He has directed the Streisand specials, the Sinatra specials and many others.

They also added announcer Gene Rayburn to the program. It was a tough assignment for Rayburn. He was a comedian, coming off an unsuccessful morning show called *Rayburn and Finch*. On the Allen show he was to be the straight announcer who did the news and weather reports, and straight lines when asked to join in.

There was also Bobby Byrne and his orchestra and a seventeen-year-old boy singer named Steve Lawrence. Lawrence was an Allen discovery; he had used him on an earlier radio show.

Within a few weeks they also added a girl singer named Eydie Gorme. "I discovered both Steve and Eydie," Allen once cracked. "I discovered them one night in the back seat of a car."

Nobody knew what was going to happen on those early late night shows, especially Allen. Because of that "who's-up what's-up?" attitude, Johnny Sterns couldn't keep up with the program and had to leave it within weeks. In his place, Dwight Hemion recommended Bill Harbach. He was the son of Otto Harbach, one of the country's most famous music writers, and he could get his father and other composers on the show as guests. Hemion understated when he said, "Bill talks funny, too."

One time, talking to Steve's agent, Harbach moaned, "Jules, for once you're wrong again."

Another time, when asked why he was sitting around with his overcoat on, Bill said, "I forgot to take it off. No. I forgot to go home," and he ran out of the office.

When he wanted that "Hollywood swimmer" he asked for Ethel Waters instead of Esther Williams. And he once excused himself from a script conference by saying, "Let me be right back."

On hand also was a young ex-*Broadway Open House* comedy writer named Stan Burns. Burns had as much to do with the early success of the Steve Allen New York show as anybody. (In later years he also had as much to do with successful television shows for Abe Burrows, Victor Borge, Smothers Brothers, Milton Berle and Carol Burnett as anybody.)

The combination of this particular Burns and Allen team plus Hemion and Harbach made eleven till midnight New York's best show in town.

It was, at the least, spontaneous.

One night Allen played the piano in his pajamas because he was "ready to go to bed as soon as the show was over."

Other times he had a barber come in and cut his hair during the show or ate his meals while the camera was on him or had a tooth filled or underwent a complete physical.

Steve's press agent, a round-bellied talker named Jim Moran, came on once a week—usually with a stuffed animal—which he claimed to have caught while crossing Central Park. One night it was a stuffed bearcat. Another night it was a live boa constrictor.

Like Garroway on the *Today Show*, Allen used the cameras and the equipment and the crew as props, wasn't afraid to have one camera shoot another or let the audience in on backstage talk, planning or even mistakes as they happened.

At first, name guests were difficult to attract. Bill Harbach helped. Raised in the household of one of America's most famous composers, young Bill had grown up knowing many famous musical people. To do "young Bill" a favor, people like Harold Arlen, Johnny Mercer and Richard Rodgers appeared as guests, on the Allen show. Soon other song writers, then song performers, then just performers, then writers, producers and other celebrities wanted to appear on the show. About this time Jules Green started another

Tonight Show tradition. Green was now Steve Allen's full-time manager and the financial manager of the program. Faced with a budget of eleven thousand dollars to do five and three quarters hours of television a week, Green decided that the show could only pay guests a flat union scale fee for being on the program. There wasn't enough money to pay stars their going rates for guest appearances, so everyone was treated the same. When *Tonight* first went on the air the scale for appearances on a program of this type was about $240. Later, on the Carson show, the rates went up to $320 for the 105-minute show, but back to $290 when the program was shorter.

One ex-director of the *Tonight Show* scoffs, however, and says, "That doesn't count hotels, food, booze, airline tickets and gifts they give some people. And it definitely doesn't count the three, even four thousand dollars a guest I've seen paid to some of them. Naturally, they don't want that news out." Offbeat guests sometimes cost more. It takes a favorable offer to attract a personality like Willie Sutton, who stole things and escaped from jails.

When he was stuck for material, Steve Allen returned to basics and went to the comfortable and familiar.

Q: I saw you waving at the camera. Who are you waving at?
A: My brother.
Q: When did you see him last?
A: At supper.

And he did bright new material:
"Tonight's bebop fable is about Jack and the Beanstalk and the Goose that was Fort Knox with feathers, for sure."

He played piano, sometimes talking through the lyrics, sometimes singing them, sometimes doing his own material or Mercer's or Hammerstein's or Harbach, Sr.'s. Steve or Eydie or both would do a song. And with the commercials, the station breaks, and the intros and the good nights, the forty minutes (later an hour) would suddenly be over, leaving music in the ears, a tickling in the ribs, and a good feeling in the people who put on the show and the people who watched it.

One out-of-town visitor wrote, "I had heard about this great Steve Allen show but I had to come to New York to see for myself how funny it really was."

If he had stayed home another month, the show would have come to him.

☆ **5**

"Can you do it?" Pat Weaver asked. "Can you do an hour
and forty-five minutes, five nights a week, more or less ad
lib?"

"Well, you know, ad-libbing is easier than it looks," Steve
Allen answered. "We do it all day long, Pat. When you go
into a butcher shop, do you have any trouble with the opening
line?"

It was September 1954. There were now thirty-one million
sets in the United States. For over three years the NBC
television network had been out of the late night program
business. When *Broadway Open House* died in August of
1951, the NBC-owned and -operated stations and the NBC
affiliated stations had rummaged among dusty film cans and
Hollywood and New York package syndicators to come up
with eighth reruns of the *Cisco Kid* or sixth showings on

One Million B.C. (Both could be turned off with the just developed Zenith remote control.)

The NBC network went off the air just after the news. Just after the weather and the sports, everything went dark at 30 Rockefeller Plaza.

The brightest spot in the dark was on WNBT, the NBC-owned and -operated station in New York. It was the Knickerbocker Beer-sponsored *Steve Allen Show* and as this local show kept more and more viewers awake it gave more and more network program people insomnia.

With the *Today Show* a success and the afternoon women's service show, *Home*, well under way, Pat Weaver decided he could now find the time and the talent to turn those dark hours into golden hours. He had the people he needed:

He had a clever planner named Richard Pinkham to put in as executive producer. Pinkham had come from the New York *Herald Tribune* to NBC in 1951 as manager of planning for the network. He had taken over as executive producer for the *Today Show* in August 1952 and had helped that show get to the top in ratings and in revenue. When the *Home Show* went on the air, Weaver had made sure that Pinkham was executive producer of that property too. The executive producer represented the network's interest.

He had a smart television programmer named Mort Werner to put in as producer. Werner had proved himself as the actual on-the-set producer for the *Today* and *Home* shows and had given them the polish and the flair and the popular appeal that Pinkham and Weaver wanted.

He had, or could get, Steve Allen and the Steve Allen format and cast.

He had a witty young station relations man named Alan Courtney to put in as the network representative to the show. His job was to handle any friction between the program, the network and the sponsors. He was also to see that the commercials were handled carefully, delivered properly and charged for profitably.

Now all Weaver needed were some stations and some advertisers.

In late July of that year Weaver announced the *Tonight Show* to his stations through a closed-circuit telecast and to the world through his press department:

"Just as NBC pioneered the way into early morning television more than two years ago with *Today*, into women's service information programs on network TV with *Home*, we are now going to stimulate new interest and enthusiasm in late evening viewing with the *Tonight Show*," Weaver said.

He went on to say that the program would be sold to smaller advertisers under the successful "magazine" plan in which they could buy one spot without sponsoring the entire show. He also said that *Tonight* would cover Broadway openings, that it would have mobile-unit remote shows from Chicago, from Hollywood, from Cleveland, from New Orleans, that the show was offered to all NBC stations as far west as Omaha and that each half hour could carry a five-minute hole to be filled with local news, sports, weather and local commercials.

He used Groucho Marx's description of Steve, "the best Allen since Fred," to describe the new host of the show. And he concluded by saying that although *Tonight* had been on the planning boards for several years at NBC, the final idea to schedule it came from the affiliates, who expressed eagerness for a major "live" late evening network show.

Most of the affiliates were not all that eager. Their reason: money.

NBC could really only muscle their five owned and operated stations into taking the *Tonight Show*. One of them, WNBT, already had it. Other NBC affiliates at the time saw *Tonight* as a move on the part of the network to move in on their income. The original network plan was to sell four one-minute commercials every half hour. These would be seen on all the stations carrying the show. Each station carrying the commercials would receive some compensation for the time. Then, every half hour, the local station could have five minutes of its own for news and local commercials and could keep all of the money from the local commercials.

It looked like a losing proposition. For the past three years, the local stations had been renting or buying reruns of *Boston Blackie* or *Housekeeper's Daughter*, selling commercials in them to the local used-car dealer and the feed and grain store and the tool-of-a-thousand-uses pitchmen and keeping all of the income, except the rental cost of the film.

NBC had tough sailing and selling ahead of it.

"They should call this one *Broadway Closed House*," one salesman said.

"*Tonightmare*," another one called it.

But on September 27, 1954, at 11:30 P.M. EST, an engineer flipped a switch at an NBC studio and viewers in thirty-three cities saw automobiles stacked up in New York's Times Square, watched the news roll around the New York Times building on the traveling sign ("Racial segregation Supreme Court decision"), saw a mounted cop, a hot-dog stand, heard the theme music, saw the titles and witnessed the on-camera birth of the first late night television program to be actually called *Tonight*.

It was *Broadway Open House*. It was *Today*. It was Steve Allen. It was familiar. But it was different too.

Steve Allen was still at "home base," the crew's name for his work area. Bill Harbach had hired a co-producer to help him, an intense, talented choreographer named Nick Vanoff. The writer, Stan Burns, had hired a gangling, taciturn ex-Marine named Herb Sargent to help him with skits. Eydie Gorme and Steve Lawrence were still with the show, but the producers had added another girl singer named Pat Marshall and a toothy, young male singer who had been part of the Kay Williams act at the Blue Angel night club. His name was Andy Williams.

They also added the Hudson Theatre, an abandoned legitimate house on the west side of Broadway, as the home studio for the *Tonight Show*. The theatre was set up with cameras, transmission equipment, cables, lights, a piano, music stands, microphones and room enough for an audience ("Sleeps eight hundred," Allen once said) on the first floor and in the balcony. It also came equipped with a ladder which Allen later used to climb into the balcony for his audience interviews.

In the rear part of the theatre the *Tonight* offices were set up and Jules Green, Steve Allen, Stan Burns, Herb Sargent, assorted musicians, Skitch Henderson, Andy Williams, Pat Marshall, Steve Lawrence, Eydie Gorme, Dwight Hemion, Bill Harbach, Nick Vanoff, Alan Courtney and a half dozen others gathered five days a week to work out the hour-and-forty-five-minute show. The odd length of the program was dictated by the Ruppert Brewery's strong refusal to give up *their Steve Allen Show*. It was all right with them if Allen went network at eleven-thirty but they wanted their Allen in their post-eleven time slot. The solution was to have Steve do a full opening and a complete fifteen-minute program with celebrities for WNBT and New York exclusively, introduce a commercial break, and then come back and do the opening again for the new network audience that had joined the show at eleven-thirty.

The first couple of nights there was general confusion. One time they lost a mobile unit out on Broadway. Another time they lost the sound while Eydie Gorme was singing a duet with Steve Lawrence. They stumbled around tripping over props, over cables, over the script, over guests and over each other. Although it was somewhat the same program, everything about it was new.

The idea of having four singers, for example. That was new. When NBC decided to put the program on the network they suggested to Steve and to Dwight and to Bill Harbach that they replace Steve and Eydie with "two better-known singers."

The *Tonight* regulars said no. The network insisted. The

Tonight people said no again. The network said they could have anybody they wanted. The *Tonight* people considered it, tongue in cheek, finally said, "Okay, we'll take Frank Sinatra and Dinah Shore."

Steve and Eydie stayed.

There were new advertisers at $4500 per minute. There were Helene Curtis, Broil-Quik, Chevrolet, Westclox, and the new picture-in-a-minute Polaroid camera which was the first sponsor to buy the network *Tonight Show*.

Many people associated with the program made money out of the Polaroid camera, some did not. When the new product was brought to the show by its agency, Doyle Dane Bernbach, the cast and crew were amazed at the picture-in-a-minute claim of the camera. Some, like Pinkham and Steve Allen, said, "I-know-a-good-thing-when-I-see-it," and immediately invested in Polaroid common stock. Value of the stock went wild. Pinkham admits, "I've been giving money away from that stock to schools and churches and charities ever since I bought it and I still have more than I started with."

By the third show, things were running along fairly well. Within the hour and forty-five minutes, Allen interviewed June Haver and Fred MacMurray, Judy Garland, her agent-husband Sid Luft, and motion picture producer Jack Warner. There had been a remote pickup from the Broadway theatre where the remake of *A Star Is Born* was being premiered and Steve Allen had even found time to do a couple of songs and to go into his studio audience and offer them an assortment of strange prizes: cast-iron pajamas for the man who tosses in his sleep, a police record for the man who feels unwanted, and a chocolate-covered hard-boiled egg on a stick.

There was also a midnight five-minute news roundup by announcer Gene Rayburn. Richard Pinkham's original idea for the show had been more like *Today*. More Rayburn and less Allen. He felt that the *Today Show* format was ideal for transfer to late night and that Steve Allen could easily imitate the slow, relaxed attitude of *Today's* Dave Garroway. Allen and, as it turned out, Weaver felt the show should be light, musical, entertaining. For a period, Pinkham and Allen fought almost daily about the approach to the program. Allen, backed by Weaver, finally won.

From the beginning, Steve and Herb Sargent and Stan Burns were determined to get the audience hooked, to make watching a nightly habit. One way to do it was with unusual show openings. They would stand there in the backstage of the Hudson Theatre, with their craziness, and dream up stunts to get the show talked about and watched.

One night the camera caught Burns and Sargent dressed as frogmen coming out of the sidewalk on a freight elevator. "It's the *Tonight Show*," one of them said through his mask.

Another night they had the camera start on one side of Broadway, look across the street through the cars, cross the opposite sidewalk and slowly search the huge building on the other side. Way up, outside of a window, they found a man drawing *The Tonight Show* on a window with a window washer's squeegee. The man was Steve Allen.

They also had Allen out in the street selling hot dogs from a cart, running a streetside beer garden, frying eggs in a thirteen-foot frying pan and staging fake car accidents. They once dressed him as a policeman and had him flag down traffic to see if the cars had any "fruits or nuts before crossing the border." Another time, Allen stood on a corner, waved down a cab, opened the rear door, threw a huge salami in it, slammed the door and yelled, "Grand Central Station and step on it!" The cab sped off.

Sometimes Allen would just sit, noodling out a melody on the piano, and deliver a musing monologue on the state of something or somewhere.

On New York, he picked out, "I'll take Manhattan," said, ". . . Radio City Music Hall seats 6200, half of whom are ushers. . . . The orchestra is the largest and the screen is seventy by forty feet. The stage cost more than $400,000 and has three seventy-foot sections. I'm telling you all this because you can't get in.

". . . New York has a severe housing shortage," he continued. "There is one choice place though, right in the heart of the gay lights, the fine restaurants and night clubs. It's located at 278th Street and Broadway, only two steps away from Canada.

"And, remember, if you come from Minnesota by car, you will find convenient parking places in Pennsylvania."

Within a month, the *Tonight Show* was the place to be for entertainers. Liz Taylor, Van Johnson, Peter Lawford, Bob and Ray, Ronnie Graham, Woody Herman, Stan Freeman and Bennett Cerf all appeared in one typical week.

That was also the week of the first network author-with-book plug on the *Tonight Show*. Bennett Cerf talked about his new book, *Anthology of American Humor*, and noticed what a good television plug could do for sales. In later years, books like Erich Segal's *Love Story* and Dr. David Reuben's *Everything You Always Wanted to Know*, etc., and Dr. Stillman's proliferating diet books would literally be taken from anonymity to best sellers through television talk-show plugs and appearances. During his period as host of the *Tonight Show*, Allen had many authors on camera to discuss their new books. Some of the authors and better sellers pushed by the show were James Michener and *The Bridges at Toko-ri*, Ben Hecht and *Child of the Century*, Major Donald Keyhoe, U.S.A.F. Ret., and *Flying Saucers from Outer Space* and Joseph Dineen and *The Anatomy of a Crime*, the best-selling book about the famous 1950 Brink's armored truck robbery.

Guests were divided into five types.

There were the big-name performers who came on and did their acts.

There were big-name performers who came on as talkers only.

There were up-and-coming performers who needed the program as a showcase for their talents.

There were serious-faced men and women with messages about charities, about books, about society.

And there were the "kooks": a collection of strange and odd human beings who were booked onto the *Tonight Show* for laughs.

The show carried a talent seeker who did nothing but book the "unusuals." He was nicknamed the "Prince of Darkness" because of the people he found. Herb Sargent swears the Prince had an inside spy in the psychiatric ward at New York's Bellevue Hospital who would tip him off when an interesting crazy was about to be released.

Once they had a man who had saved up ten thousand pounds of chicken bones. Another man was going to parachute from the top of the Empire State Building. Another put his hand in a bowl full of piranha fish. Another tried to lift an elephant. One almost turned out tragically. Allen decided it would be fascinating to interview a convicted rapist and had his crew book one. The network turned it down. When the rapist was told he was canceled, he threatened to kill Allen on sight.

And along with them came the others: the Kelly Family from Philadelphia including daughter-movie-star Grace, Art Linkletter, Carl Sandburg, Salvador Dali, Burl Ives, Faye Emerson, Milton Berle, the Seven Little Foys, Duke Ellington, Fred Allen, Elsa Lanchester, Margaret Truman, and one memorable night they had Zsa Zsa Gabor on for her first of what must by now be five hundred *Tonight Show* appearances. A little later, prophetically, they had Debbie Reynolds and Eddie Fisher on to talk about the problems of show-business marriages. For their appearances, all of the Mr. and Misses Wonderful and Mr. and Misses Wacko were paid scale and not a cent more by producer Jules Green.

Allen and his people did some of the earliest "single" shows. They did the first single guest, Carl Sandburg. ("How

do you interrupt Carl Sandburg reading his *Lincoln* to say it's
time for a commercial?") They did single-subject shows. One
was on Negro music and musicians. Another was on the culture and arts of Israel. They put together a program on
narcotics with interviews of masked junkies, displays of equipment used by narcotics addicts, films on withdrawal, and an
interview with Dr. Nathaniel Cooper, director of health of
the New York City Health and Welfare Commission. That
was in early 1955. They did one on the pros and cons of the
then-popular exposé magazines and had the publisher of
Confidential on the show. They did shows on brotherhood,
on civil rights, on crime, on The Bomb. One of the "confrontation" shows which attracted much attention was about
AWARE, an organization set up to "expose Communists and
leftist members of the acting profession."

Inspiration for the show came from a column written by
columnist John Crosby for the New York *Herald Tribune*. In
that column, Crosby called AWARE a secret police outfit,
said that it prevented people from working through use of
smear and innuendo, that the blacklists contained individuals
purely because they had foreign names, because they appeared in playwright Arthur Miller's plays or had once
marched in a freedom-type parade. He blasted the Borden
Company (sponsors of a show called *Justice*) for dropping
an actor whose only crime was having the same name as a
blacklisted actor and he praised Kraft, Philco, Goodyear and
CBS for telling AWARE vigilantes to go chase their tales.

At the Hudson Theatre and at each other's throats that
night were Godfrey P. Schmidt, president of AWARE and an
associate professor of constitutional law at Fordham University, and Vincent W. Hartnett, one of the authors of
Red Channels, a book that reportedly listed the Communists
and Communist-front groups in the entertainment industry.

Facing them on the panel were a handsome blonde actress
and television personality named Faye Emerson and the
Herald Tribune columnist John Crosby.

The network had been terrified of the confrontation and had tried until the last moment to get Allen off the subject or, as they thought, they would be off the air. Instead, mail poured in that was overwhelmingly opposed to indictment by slander and NBC and Steve Allen learned that the *Tonight Show* could successfully depart from its fun and games routine to handle serious subject matter.

This was a time of change for Steve Allen. He had met and married a lovely television actress named Jayne Meadows. Within the security of the new *Tonight Show* success and the flourishing new marriage, Allen found time to read and to think. He pored through Thomas Merton's *Seven Storey Mountain*, through Thomas Paine's *The Age of Reason*, through Bertrand Russell, Thomas Aquinas, Edward Gibbon, Will Durant and the classic philosophers. He began reading regular issues of the *National Review*, a conservative publication, and the *Daily Worker*, a Communist paper, just to exercise his personal judgment.

Commenting on this new input, he said, "I'm really disturbed by a world where people buy booze but not books." He described himself as a "radical middle-of-the-roader" and soon got himself involved in the movements to ban atmospheric nuclear bomb testing and to defend the United Nations and to keep up the good battle for civil rights.

"I'm not worried about my TV rating," he said to NBC when they were concerned about the AWARE confrontation, "I am worried about mankind's rating."

During that time and, of course, since, Allen has become known as a brilliant man of many talents. To date, he has written and published twelve books ranging from the bittersweet but very funny autobiographical *Mark It and Strike It*, to a novel, *Not All of Your Laughter, Not All of Your Tears*, to a political treatise on migratory labor called *The Ground Is Our Table*. He has some forty record albums to his credit and has written well over three thousand songs, at a rate of from three to ten a week. He's written the title lyrics for the film hits *On the Beach*, *Houseboat*, *Sleeping Beauty*, and *Bell, Book and Candle*. A play about his childhood entitled *The Wake* opened to smash reviews in California and was last seen headed east toward Broadway.

From that first confrontation, the *Tonight Show* audience saw the sober, serious Allen from time to time. Quite often they couldn't tell if he was serious or not. One night he began talking about the U. S. Immigration Department and how they wouldn't let immigrants bring important personal possessions into the country—like salamis.

"Here are a few smuggling hints, however, to you people on Ellis Island with your salamis. Wear a pair of open-toed salamis. Tell customs men your salami is a flat clarinet. Slice one up as arch supporters. Put a buckle on it and wear it as a money belt. Stamp it as a two iron or put a fox head on it and say it's a fur piece. . . ."

Another time he was talking to a crime expert about gunshot wounds and said, "I once knew a man who was shot through the heart and lived to be ninety-six."

The guest was amazed.

"Yep," said Steve, "turned ninety-six a minute after he was shot."

One of Allen's funniest show spots was "working the audience." He would take a hand microphone, climb the ladder into the balcony of the Hudson Theatre and talk to people sitting there, just as he had that night long ago in Hollywood when he discovered people were the funniest material of all.

Working with them and giving out odd gifts, Allen soon developed a group of regulars who were so funny that writers of other shows often said they were ringers and actors in disguise. One of the steadiest was Mrs. Sterling, who seemed to have no home other than on-the-aisle at the Hudson Theatre. During the two years of the network *Tonight Show*, Allen loaded her down with salami, watches, perfumes and appliances. Not content with the gifts lavished on her, Mrs. Sterling continually asked for a second gift for her daughter. Sometimes Allen gave her a second gift, sometimes he asked that Mrs. Sterling's daughter come in to get it herself. Whether there actually was a Mrs. Sterling's daughter was never revealed.

An upstate New York farmer, John Schafer, accidentally became the *Tonight Show's* movie reviewer for a period. One night he had described a film called *Mogambo* this way: ". . . it sure was something when those old gorillas came running around and old Clark [Gable] had to step lively to keep things on an even keel."

There was Ben Belefonte, the rhyming inventor who came up with new ideas like a savings bank made out of a wooden hanger. There was Joe Interleggi, who opened bottles with his teeth and who ate wood. Allen once called him The Human Termite. And there was Miss Dorothy Miller, who followed Allen from Hollywood to New York and showed up at his program faithfully. She also showed up when the program did remotes—in Niagara Falls, Hollywood, Havana, Texas. She became such a steady on the Allen show . . . and later on the Jack Paar show . . . that the American Federation of Television and Radio Artists, the guild which controls actors on live television, forced her to join the union.

Sometimes he combined laughter and tears. On the night of March 19, 1956, the entire *Tonight Show* was dedicated to the late comedian Fred Allen. Within the framework of the program, Allen had many greats from show business join in a eulogy to a man they had all admired. Among other people at the New York studio or the Hollywood cut-in portions were publisher Bennett Cerf, motion picture executive Howard Dietz, novelist Herman Wouk (who had been a gag writer for Fred Allen), Jack Benny, Bob Hope, plus kinescopes and films of Fred Allen with Clifton Webb, Libby Holman, Dave Garroway, Pinky Lee, Groucho Marx and the regulars on the old *Allen's Alley* radio show including Kenny Delmar, who played Senator Claghorn, and Peter Donald, who had played Ajax Cassidy, and Parker Fennelly, who had played Titus Moody. The program closed with Steve Allen reading from Fred Allen's book, *Treadmill to Oblivion*; a book about the insanities of television.

On another occasion, Steve Allen took to his podium to praise a labor columnist named Victor Riesel and to attack labor racketeering. Riesel had been blinded by an acid-throwing hood on the streets of New York and Allen took the story of this brave man to the public, damned the acid thrower and the men who paid him to do it. He warned Americans to start cleaning up their unions or more and more of this might-is-right would become the labor unions' methods.

The telephone calls began coming in.

"Lay off, pal, or you're next."

To show him they weren't kidding, they set off stink bombs in the audience one night.

"They could have been real bombs," somebody said.

Another night, Allen went outside after the show and found the tires of his car had been slashed.

"Could have been your face," somebody said.

Although shaken by these incidents, Allen shrugged them off, continued to do a fast-paced, interesting show every night, five nights a week. It was funny most of the time, serious when he wanted it to be.

From the very beginning Harbach found that remote broadcasts—telecasts from out of studio locations—managed to attract large home audiences. They did one remote from a Broadway jazz club called Birdland and they did one from the ice skating rink in Rockefeller Center and they did one from the Luxor Baths in New York, trying to keep the nude cigar-chewing steam-room guests out of camera range. They did a salute to railroads from the Baltimore & Ohio Railroad roundhouse in Baltimore. They did shows from a rodeo in Fort Worth, from a newspaper plant, from the Museum of Modern Art, from the roller derby, from Grauman's Chinese Theatre in Hollywood, and from the "invasion" beaches of downtown Miami Beach. . . .

The *Today Show* with Dave Garroway had decided to do some remote telecasts from Florida. To save money and spread out its investment in travel and transmission setups, NBC officials suggested that the *Tonight Show* originate from Miami Beach at the same time. Co-producer Nick Vanoff and the writers were then trying to top themselves nightly with ideas for the show opening.

"I know!" one of them said. "Let's have a full invasion of the beach by the Marines."

"Huh?"

"Then when the guns go off and the landing craft come in and the troops swarm ashore and the tracer bullets light up the sky, the announcer can yell, 'The *Tonight Show!*' eh, guys?"

Vanoff got the short straw, had to call the Marines and ask them if they would invade a section of Miami Beach's posh hotel shoreline and since the show was live, the landing would have to be done at eleven-thirty at night, thank you. (During this time the government found it acceptable to loan out military units for private films or television showings or public appearances. Milton Berle had recently originated a telecast from the deck of a Navy aircraft carrier and the Marines were looking for equal time or publicity.)

What Vanoff and the writers had nearly forgotten was that one of the early Israel-Arab crises was going on and Miami Beach was (a) full of the news and (b) full of Jews who were understandably nervous about the threatened warfare.

Without warning, late one night the landing lights flashed on, the landing sirens whined, tracer bullets plowed into the sand, buried powder charges exploded, landing craft crunched into the sand and yelling Marines came splashing ashore in full combat gear with the cameras grinding and the big television lights glaring and the smoke spreading over all.

Hysteria hit several blocks of hotels. Guests screamed or ran up and down corridors with no clothes on yelling, "The

Arabs have landed!" One guest jumped from the third floor of his hotel into the hotel pool. Another came running into the scene brandishing his cane at a fully armed Marine. A group on one of the hotel balconies turned a fire hose on an advancing squad of Marines but scattered, shrieking, when the Marines fired blanks at them.

After it was all over and the guests had been told that it was "those *meshugana* show people from New York" and soothed and settled down, and the scandal of the invasion was fairly well hushed up in the Miami press, the *Today* and *Tonight* shows packed up their lights, camera, and mostly their action and—by popular demand—headed back to New York.

The Allen show didn't have to go to Miami Beach to try new adventures. They created many right outside the studio door.

One night they just aimed a lit camera out the doorway and had Allen make comments about the people who looked into the camera from the street.

Another night, Steve read a letter which said that Allen reminded the writer of Clark Kent in his owlish, dark-rimmed-glasses way. The writers and Allen decided to make a skit out of it.

They had Allen go into the street, hear a cry for help, and then decide to become Superman and save the damsel in distress. Allen went into a telephone booth there on the corner by the Hudson Theatre and closed the door and began to peel off his clothing to reveal the Superman costume underneath. Allen is six feet two inches tall and a hundred and ninety-five pounds large and the telephone booth was too small for complete undressing. He had his shirt half off, was trying to get his pants off, and was imprisoned in both.

Looking for help, he waved at a stranger who was walking by.

"Hey, you, come here," yelled Allen.

"Me?"

"Yeah, you. Come here. Say, fella, would you help me get my pants off?"

"Huh?"

"My pants. Help me get them off. See, I'm Superman and there's a girl in distress and I have to go help her."

Unaware of the camera or the camera crew taking it all in, the stranger said, "Sure," helped Allen get undressed, wished him luck and went on his way, acting as though nothing unusual had happened. Even when Allen went flying by him, supported by wires on a hidden belt, the stranger waved, smiled, continued walking.

This kind of supersophistication always stumped Allen and his writers. They noticed that people would react to the most unlikely situations yet not be disturbed by the most obvious scenes. In a later show, Allen attacked the Hollywood Ranch Market, an open-fronted, giant supermarket across the street from his Hollywood studio. While dozens of people poured through the store yelling, "Attack!" and "Charge!" and threw apples and oranges as hand grenades, the shoppers continued picking out cans, selecting meats and checking out as though the store was deserted.

The *Tonight Show* did so many remotes that Allen kidded his audience about it. "One of these nights we're going to come to you from a uranium mine and after the show they're going to seal us in. Or we may originate in a Las Vegas casino where we would lose the network to Nick the Greek. Or perhaps we will do one in Washington, D.C., before the Justice Department where we will all be jailed for life. Or from Rome where they will throw us into the Coliseum with seven hundred and fifty starving American actors."

One of the craziest shows ever originated under the *Tonight* name was done on October 5, 1955. It had as guests Leona Anderson, who was billed as "the world's worst singer," eight real train announcers, someone called Mad Mogi, Rose Mackenburg, who was an exposer of spiritualists, Miss Human Christmas Tree, two survivors of the *Titanic*, and Henry

Krajewski, who was a pig farmer from New Jersey and a candidate for the Presidency of the United States.

The show also originated the famous Crazy Shots sequences. These were visual gags, sight puns and other unique setups, usually set to background music. Later, Ernie Kovacs was to use this technique extensively on his shows and, much later, the *Laugh-In* producers went the second time around with a lot of the Allen and Kovacs material.

A typical *Tonight Show* Crazy Shots sequence would start with Allen at the piano playing a melody. The camera would go in very tight on his ear and hold the picture, then cut away to goldfish in the water cooler, then to an oven with two bare feet sticking out of it, a headless woman, and then to human hands pointing out time on the face of a clock.

The *Tonight Show* also began turning the cameras over to new comedy talents. Mort Sahl came on with his "I'd rather be right than President which is the way we do it in this country" routines. Lenny Bruce was invited on and didn't say one dirty word. Shelley Berman, Tim Conway, Mike Nichols and Elaine May, Jim Nabors, Don Adams, the Smothers Brothers, Jackie Mason, Jackie Vernon and others all came on, did their turns as guests—many for the first time on television—and went on to become top comics.

In addition to the guest comedians, Allen began developing his own group of regulars: Louis Nye, Tom Poston, Don Knotts, Bill Dana, all of whom were given strong characterizations by Allen's writers, Stan Burns and Herb Sargent. Several of these comedians admit that the days of working with Allen (during the *Tonight Show* and later, on Allen's Sunday evening show) were the highlights of their careers and their personal popularity. When they left the Allen "Man-On-The-Street" format, they settled back into relative or near total obscurity.

Although the program remained hard to sell to advertisers for the first year, the home audience loved it.

In a year when *The George Gobel Show*, William Bendix

in *The Life of Riley* and the *Adventures of Ozzie and Harriet* were the top-rated shows, Steve Allen's *Tonight Show* became one of the most talked-about and watched programs.

The New York City Young Men's Board of Trade voted Steve Allen the Outstanding Young Man of the Year. Others who had been previously honored included baseball players Jackie Robinson and Lou Gehrig, and a district attorney named Thomas E. Dewey.

The Gilbert Youth Research Poll found that Allen was the favorite television personality of America's teen-agers, proving that what the ad agencies said was partially true— that only kids and swing workers and insomniacs stayed up to watch Allen.

But the show began to sell, began to get ratings, began to prosper. Allen had started out at $3000 a week on the program. By 1956 he was making $5000 a week and before the show went off the air he was making $10,000 a week for his late-hour all-American hash of *commedia dell' arte* and vaudeville and town hall of the air.

The *Tonight Show* was now costing NBC about $42,000 a week to produce and commercials were up to $6700 a minute from their original $4500 asking price.

During the next two and a half years, many unrehearsed incidents happened that the survivors of the show still talk about . . . sometimes with astonishment, sometimes with a chuckle, sometimes with sheer disbelief that they happened at all.

One night when Dwight Hemion, the director, went on vacation, Alan Courtney and Nick Vanoff and Bill Harbach decided to give a young director a chance on the show. He had seemed pleasant and talented and even Hemion had said he would be good.

The young director put the show on the air and began calling camera shots, changing scenes, getting set up for the next move. He had Steve Allen smoothly into and out of skits, had the singers in the right spots and the musicians ready to go on cue, snapped the commercials into place exactly on time and was directing a tight, fast-paced, skillfully assembled show. It was twelve-forty when he said into the microphone, "Stand by for signoff."

"Hey, whaddaya mean stand by for signoff, it's only twelve-forty," said Courtney, pointing to the studio clock.

"Guess it is, Alan," said the director, smiling, "but that's all the show I've got." And so that night the eleven-thirty-to-one *Tonight Show* signed off promptly at twelve-forty.

One year Steve Allen sent a memo to the cast and crew saying he wanted no Christmas gifts from any of them. Back came a handsomely wrapped and tied gift from Stan Burns and Herb Sargent. It was his no-gift memo, carefully and expensively framed.

One night they were doing a program for the Lighthouse for the Blind. Without thinking, somebody had programmed the popular song, "I Only Have Eyes for You" for a duet. Producer Vanoff changed it just in time.

Another night, producer Bill Harbach wanted to get the vaudeville comedy team of Fric and Frac on the show. He yelled at an assistant, "Get me those guys, uh, Trick or Treat."

After singer Pat Marshall married a very talented comedy writer named Larry Gelbart (one of the writers of *A Funny Thing Happened on the Way to the Forum*) she was replaced by a petite brunette named Pat Kirby. Several months later, *Tonight* did a full-show salute to composer Richard Rodgers. They did selections from *Victory at Sea*, from *Oklahoma*, from *Pal Joey*, from *Carousel*, from *The King and I*, from other Richard Rodgers masterpieces. As the show was getting ready to sign off, Rodgers stood backstage talking with one of the producers. He mentioned that he was very taken with Pat Kirby's ability and would like to buy her a drink or a cup of coffee to see if she'd be interested in starring in his next show.

"Gee, that's very nice, but I can't," said Pat Kirby, "I have a date with my boy friend."

"That's what you call a real no-show," Courtney cracked.

Herb Sargent, one of the writers, decided it would be fun to have Broadway star Tallulah Bankhead on the show. She was staying with friends in a remote northeastern village but a group decided to call on her. She had a buffet laid out, offered the group a drink, and they sat around chatting for a moment. The *Tonight* people talked about the program. Bankhead talked about people she knew who had been or should be guests on it. During the conversation she mentioned one of her dear friends, a famous theatrical personality.

One of the writers had been sitting there taking it all in, listening quietly, but the mention of this man was too much for him.

"Miss Bankhead, uh, Tallulah," he interrupted. "Listen, do you mind if I ask a question? Uh, since you know him and all, I wonder . . . listen. Is it true he really, uh, really, uh, is a homosexual?"

"I don't know, dahling," the heavy-voiced Tallulah shot back. "He has never grabbed my cock."

The Broadway show *Kismet* opened during one of New York's periodic newpaper strikes. Since Broadway shows live or die on newspaper reviews, everyone connected with *Kismet* felt that the show would fold very rapidly. However, Allen and his producers had the idea of presenting musical numbers from the show on the *Tonight* program. *Kismet* stayed alive and went on to become a smash success.

They also remember when Steve Allen started to become famous. One night when he climbed into a cab the driver looked into the mirror, said, "Say, you're Steve Allen. Say, you look just like yourself."

Another time a woman rushed up to Allen on Park Avenue and said, "Would you give me your autograph, Mr. Garroway?"

"Certainly, but I'm not Dave Garroway."

"Don't tell me you're not Dave Garroway, you stuck-up thing. We'll never watch you again."

Allen's popularity had led NBC to give him a Sunday night show, one directly across from the rating king, Ed Sullivan. The demands of the Sunday night show were so tough that Allen found less and less of his time involved with the *Tonight Show* and more of his energies spent in a battle to attract some of the Sullivan audience away from CBS to NBC.

At first NBC offered help. They would, they said, take off some of his load by having another host and cast on two nights a week. They hired the cigar-chewing Hungarian, Ernie Kovacs, to take over the *Tonight Show* on Monday and Tuesday nights. Kovacs brought along Bill Wendell as the announcer, an orchestra led by Leroy Holmes, and two singers. On the first show, October 1, 1956, Kovacs did a satire on success stories, did his famous Nairobi African apes musical number, did his Percy Dovetonsils martini-drinking poet spot, did a satire on game shows, did Cinderella as Alfred Hitchcock would do it, and ended up shooting three arrows into the air which ended up in the band leader, the announcer and a comedienne on the show.

Allen strengthened his production staff, hired a total of seven writers, added cast members, but the work load began to strain the show and the host. Finally, Jules Green told NBC that Steve would have to drop the *Tonight Show*, to concentrate on the Sunday night program. NBC needed help on that Sunday night spot so they reluctantly agreed.

On January 25, 1957, the last Steve Allen *Tonight Show* went on the air. It was a farewell party and Allen reprised all of the famous jokes and devices he had used through the years. On hand to say good-by to him were Jayne Meadows, Micki Marlo, Buddy Hackett, Milt Kamin, Peter Lawford, columnist John Crosby, Sammy Davis, Jr., Lionel Hampton and Steve's favorite audience guest, Mrs. Sterling.

One columnist writing in the next day's newspaper said,

"Allen's goodbyes to his countrywide *Tonight* fans were touching—because they were from the heart, without the least sign of self-dramatization. No touch of the maudlin was in evidence, although it would have been so easy to have swung in that direction. Steve recognized . . . the deprivation his departure meant to shut-ins and the like. He said so. . . . In all likelihood he valued those fans beyond all others . . . for some time the word was around that the Allen format of *Tonight* was doomed. If he was out, so was the program. There was no one to replace him. . . ."

John Crosby wrote, "There will be a *Tonight Show* next year, but it won't be the show as we know it."

He was right.

It never was again.

"Steve Allen doing anything is a hard act to follow. Steve Allen doing everything is almost impossible," said one reviewer.

"Impossible," echoed NBC sadly.

There are hundreds of thousands, maybe millions, of people around who saw the Steve Allen *Tonight Show*. There are tens of millions around who saw the Jack Paar *Tonight Show*. And every month over 200,000,000 people watch the Johnny Carson *Tonight Show*. But probably the only people who remember seeing the *Tonight Show* produced between Steve Allen's time and Jack Paar's era are the people who were on the show and their agents and relatives.

It was called, *Tonight! America After Dark.*

It went on as a cheap-jack, makeshift replacement for Steve Allen's *Tonight Show* on the Monday following Allen's

Friday night farewell. *Tonight! America After Dark* was made up of snips and bits and pieces and dog-eared memos and groupthink and spur-of-the-moment inspirations from the programming department, from the news department, from the sales department, from the engineering department, and probably from the elevator starter at 30 Rockefeller Plaza.

Despite its success, the Steve Allen *Tonight Show* had not been the favorite of every NBC executive. The news department still felt that the program should contain some hard news coverage and mini-documentaries on the day's news. Several of the NBC executive production staff felt that Allen's format was too formless, too squirmy, too hard to handle, too easy a target for the FCC and other pressure groups. Some of the salesmen and programmers in the *Today-Home-Tonight* group felt that the *Tonight Show* should have been an exact copy of the *Today Show*—in format, in appeal, and in sales. Under Allen, the *Tonight Show* had been a collection of musical numbers, comedy skits, ad libs, offbeat guests, audience interviews, remote broadcasts, book and music reviews, discussions, and an over-all feeling of laughter, of zaniness, of gaiety and good spirits.

The *Today Show* was profiled as a more sincere, more somber, straight-talking, eye-to-eye confrontation with the gloomy gray dawn and the day ahead.

Too, one programming executive pointed out that personalities like Steve Allen left NBC impotent when they walked out, died or moved to another network. The audiences were loyal to the personality and not the program and that was a trap that NBC shouldn't allow itself to walk into again.

The programming department writhed about like a headless snake—waiting for the late night hours to die. The head was gone because NBC's house genius, Pat Weaver, was gone. Just before Steve Allen cut his five-a-week to three-a-week, Weaver and the younger Sarnoff had faced off in a Board of

Directors meeting. The directors sided with Robert and Weaver was out, effective right then.

"The day of the Big Think is over!" one of Sarnoff's people jubilantly reported.

"Yes, it is," a Weaver man softly replied.

Three months or so after Weaver's run-in with Sarnoff, Steve Allen closed down his *Tonight Show*. There was now a huge hole in the programming department and in the late night programming.

Shuffling the memos, the suggestions, the meetings, the letters, the conferences, the schedules, the availabilities and the ideas, NBC programming management came up with a new approach to late night television. It was planned to retain the old Steve Allen *Tonight Show* audience and to add millions to it because of a "broader appeal."

Tonight! America After Dark was assembled as a late night variety and special features program which borrowed its attitudes from the *Today Show* and its style from *Wide, Wide World*. There were differences: this *Tonight Show* would concentrate on what America did after dark. Grand, general outlines called for the program to offer mobile-unit on-the-spot coverage that captured the tempo and pacing of night life throughout the country. The program would spotlight new and undiscovered talents; it would cover all facets of the entertainment world: night clubs, jazz clubs, restaurants, theatres, sports events. It would take itself seriously at times and visit a heart disease research clinic, an atomic energy laboratory, a political rally or a tornado-crumpled town. (Within two weeks after it went on the air, mobile units interrupted the show with on-the-spot coverage of an airplane crash at Riker's Island, New York.) The program would also pack in local news, weather reports, theatre reviews, inventors, starlets, politicians, sports scores, audience games and a dozen other features originating in New York, in Chicago and in Los Angeles.

To run all of this, they picked the boy-next-dorable announcer named Jack Lescoulie. To back him up, they hired a singer-talker named Judy Johnson (about six weeks after the show started), the musical Lou Stein Trio, and six newspaper columnists in three major cities. These were to be the "feature reporters," who would work from the mobile units.

In New York, they picked Hy Gardner, Bob Considine and Earl Wilson. In Chicago they selected Irv Kupcinet. And in Los Angeles they tagged Vernon Scott and Paul Coates. Some had television shows of their own, most had heavy television experience. Because even NBC programmers realized that not all feature stories came from those three cities, the format also called for non-staff newsmen in places like New Orleans or Detroit to report in on fast-breaking or wacky news events. A few months after the program began, San Francisco became a regular reporting station and Miami Beach and Topeka had both been heard from.

The early format of the show demonstrated the concept of "something-for-everybody."

11:15—11:20   Jack Lescoulie and Constance Moore welcomed guest, began series of five-minute "teaser" switches to various remote units.

11:20—11:22   Alfred Hayes house, Brentwood, California. A remote pickup of this uniquely designed house, with a real Hollywood party going on.

11:25—11:29   Eli Wallach, in New York studio. An interview with this actor who just dropped in from his nightly appearance in Broadway's *Major Barbara.*

11:33—11:38   Beauty City, New York City. Switch to this all-night beauty parlor. Earl Wilson walked around with a microphone talking about this shop that handled people who couldn't get their hair done during the day. He interviewed the owner of Beauty City

Jack Paar and Dave Garroway

Top: Skitch Henderson

Opposite, right: Allen's TONIGHT

Right: José Melis

Sammy Davis, Jr., Frank Sinatra, Joey Bishop (substitute host)

Pat Weaver, Steve Allen

BROADWAY OPEN HOUSE: Jerry Lester,
Milton DeLugg with accordion, and Dagmar

Tiny Tim's wedding

Senator Eugene McCarthy with Johnny Carson and Jack Haskell

Bill Cosby, Muhammad Ali and Johnny Carson

and actress Dagmar, dancer Gretchen Wyler, a Copa dancer named Gwen O'Hara, and Miss Sweden.

11:38—11:46   Cut back to the studio and interview with Leonard Feather, the jazz editor of *Playboy* and author of the *Encyclopedia Yearbook of Jazz.* The other guest in the studio was trombone great J. J. Johnson, who played a number with the Lou Stein Trio. At this point, Lescoulie said, "Say, wouldn't it be great if we had all twenty-four of *Playboy's* jazz winners on *America After Dark* one at a time, then all together!"

At eleven forty-nine they cut away from all that jazz and went back to the California party to have Jolie Gabor, dancer Ann Miller and Linda Darnell tell us what a grand time they were having.

Fifteen minutes later the switcher cut Eli Wallach back in again and he did a reading from Sacha Guitry's *Debureau,* which is about a clown telling his son what it means to be an actor.

After four minutes of commercials, the cameras cut to the top of the Merchandise Mart in Chicago. Irv Kupcinet interviewed a man named Hal Connor who ran the Helitaxi port, one of the first helicopter cab services in the country. This was good for three minutes.

Back then to the Hayes house in California for five more minutes of party, then right back to Chicago, but this time, inside the Merchandise Mart at the NBC studios. Here, Kupcinet interviewed ex-world's heavyweight champion Joe Louis about his back tax bill of one million dollars. Louis ended the interview by saying it wasn't his fault he owed the money.

By now it was twelve-thirty and the cameras cut back to the New York studio and an interview with Red Auerbach, coach of the Boston Celtics pro-basketball team, and his star players, veteran Bob Cousy and newly hired Olympics star Bill Russell. This went on for six minutes.

Then two more minutes of J. J. Johnson playing more jazz.

Then six more minutes of Beauty City while the girls came out of the driers.

Then three more minutes of that increasingly drunker party in California.

And finally it was twelve fifty-six and everybody said good night.

Despite the straight men who had the *Tonight! America After Dark* format buckled down, it shifted almost nightly. Three weeks after the program went on the air the producers added "The World Tonight"—a news segment run by New York columnist Bob Considine.

A month later they gave Hy Gardner a nightly ten-minute strip called "Face to Face" in which he interviewed a personality currently in the news.

A month after that they added "Hy Gardner Time"—another five-minute filler of no great significance. One of the features on this segment was the "Look Alikes" spot. In these minutes, Gardner showed pictures of a well-known personality and an average citizen and asked the audience to guess who was which. Interestingly enough, this device or ones like it (wryly captioned photos, baby pictures, etc.) have been used steadily throughout the *Tonight Show* from Allen through Carson.

The producers of *America After Dark* juggled everything but tenpins.

They gave Considine a second news spot for a daily human interest story or editorial on the day's news.

They added a straight man-on-the-street interview.

They fired the Lou Stein Trio in March and replaced it with the Mort Lindsay Quartet. They fired the Mort Lindsay Quartet in June and replaced it with the Johnny Guarnieri Quartet. In July they fired them.

They waited for Jack Lescoulie to become Dave Garroway

or Steve Allen or even Kukla, Fran or Ollie and when he didn't they fired him the third week in June and hired another "disc jockey" (this was based on the fact that Allen had been a "disc jockey") named Al "Jazzbo" Collins who worked in a bizarre set called the Purple Grotto. He lasted from the end of June until the end of the show, which wasn't all that much longer.

The native columnists became restless, too. Within a month of going on the air, California columnist Vernon Scott quit and was replaced by Lee Giroux of the Los Angeles NBC outlet. Earl Wilson left the program in July. And that month the producers decided to visit only one city a night on remote pickup instead of three or four.

From the beginning, the great whale of *Tonight! America After Dark* flopped around, spouted foul air, and beached itself in its own shallows. Some advertisers had left the *Tonight Show* the moment Allen departed. Some waited around, on a discount basis, to see if the new format would deliver the same old or better audiences for their products. One by one they began cutting back and canceling because they didn't like the program or more importantly because the program was losing audience and slipping badly in the ratings. Before the program was finally canceled, one executive guessed it had easily chased five million dollars' worth of advertising back into magazines. (The sudden change in viewership couldn't happen today, according to Dick Pinkham. He believes that the *Tonight Show*, now, has so much momentum a chimpanzee could run it for six months without losing a viewer.)

By the time "Jazzbo" Collins had taken over for Lescoulie, the program had changed. On July 17, for example, *America After Dark* started with a singer, went to Gardner's "Face to Face" feature, another musical number, an interview with cat-care people in New York, "Hy Gardner Time," a switch to a square dance in Greenwich Village hosted by Hugh Downs, an interview with women's rights spokespeople, "The World

Tonight" news segment, man-in-the-street interviews, "Considine's Corner" and good night.

Through it all, there were no entertainment breakthroughs, no news-making incidents, no scandals or items of gossip worth mentioning, on or off the program. The members of the cast wandered through the show as if it were an NBC white paper on anesthesia. It was a big yawn and it was contagious and what viewers were left throughout the country clicked off their sets or turned back to the eighteenth rerun of *Charlie Chan-and-the-Copra-Caper.*

From the second night out—or thereabouts—NBC executives who had been so enthusiastic about the new show suddenly began to write memos disassociating themselves from the offering. There was a major scramble to abandon any involvement with it. Confident, boisterous programmers who had been saying *America After Dark* was their idea now had other shows to produce, other cities to be in, other poor fish to fry. Once again it was red alert time in the NBC programming department. Dick Linkroum, the producer, was told to get a new show and get it in that late night slot fast. The smell of panic spread. Up in Bronxville, New York, an out-of-work daytime game show host who had failed at just about everything he had ever tried sniffed one day and picked up the telephone. It was NBC calling.

Dick Linkroum made the call. It was to Jack Paar. Paar and Linkroum decided to meet. They did and talked about the new program. Paar said that although he had been out of work for some time he knew, just knew, he could make it if Linkroum would just please give him a chance. Linkroum, who was trying to clamber out of the *America After Dark* ruins, said he'd see what he could do. He suggested Paar to NBC programming head Mort Werner and the other programming executives and Werner was enthusiastic. Werner felt that Paar was good, was soft-sell enough to get the audience and the advertisers coming back. They said okay, they would hire Paar as the host of the to-be-revamped *To-*

night Show. When he was told about his new job, according to one source, Paar shouted, "That Linkroum, he's great, he's a genius, I'll always be eternally grateful to him." Six months later Paar was to totally change his attitude toward Linkroum, who was barred from the studio and eventually fired from the network.

The last showing of *Tonight! America After Dark* was on July 26, 1957. The regulars were down to "Jazzbo" Collins, singer Judy Johnson, the Guarnieri Quartet and columnists Hy Gardner and Bob Considine from New York and Paul Coates from Los Angeles.

On that last night, Gardner interviewed Dagmar, one of the original stars of *Broadway Open House*, predecessor of the *Tonight Show*. Then *Metronome* magazine's musician of the year, an accordionist named Matt Matthews, played a number. The camera switched to the West Side Manhattan apartment of Edie Adams and Ernie Kovacs to look at gold-leaf pianos, two-dollar cigars and twenty-some rooms where the velvet was cut and the costs were not. Then a cut away to California and the San Fernando swimming pool of program associate director Gordon Wiles, where people splashed, swam, sang songs and said good-by. Ah yes, there was also a magician named Richard Himber who did some magic tricks on the show.

One trick he did not try was to make the show and its cast disappear.

NBC had done that before he was booked.

☆ **7**

"He's sort of like Peter Pan if *Peter Pan* had been written by Mickey Spillane," said the network executive.

He was talking about Jack Paar, a professional television emcee and host who had been a summer replacement personality for so long, one critic said they put him away with the other nuts during the winter.

It was the spring of 1957 and NBC's newest late night show, *Tonight! America After Dark*, was becoming more and more a loser. It was losing personalities, it was losing stations, it was losing sponsors and it was losing, according to one *Newsweek* report, a million dollars in twenty-one weeks. The producer of *America After Dark*, an enthusiastic believer in nighttime programming named Dick Linkroum, was in danger of losing his NBC-derived income if he didn't come up with something to lighten the dark outlook for those dark hours.

"What we need is another Steve Allen," said one group of NBC executives.

"How about Eddie Albert and Margo?" said another.

"There's always Joey Bishop," said another.

"Always," said a fourth.

"Hey, I know. Walter Kiernan or Jerry Lewis, yeah, Jerry Lewis."

Hal March, Art Linkletter, Shelley Berman, Orson Bean, Mort Sahl, Arlene Francis, Jim Moran and several dozen others were all mentioned as the man of the hour, that hour being from eleven-thirty until one five nights a week.

It was Linkroum's job to ferret out a personality who could improvise a new show format, who could chat his way through five nights a week, attract sponsors back, get the stations in line again, and bring viewers back from the Late and Late Late Movies on other networks. Linkroum and other NBC executives ran through talent agency lists, caught night club acts, looked at kinescopes, interviewed actors, performers, personalities, before they finally agreed to hire the "I kid you not" kid, Jack Paar.

The office of Mort Werner was where the passing buck had stopped. Werner had nominated Paar because of his deft handling of past *Morning Shows* on CBS.

The *Morning Show* had been the CBS entry in the flop derby. Until Paar took it over, that program had been run by Walter Cronkite as an early news and commentary show. Paar changed it to an all-entertainment program to compete more directly with NBC's successful *Today Show* under Dave Garroway. Broadcast experts shook their heads when the new Paar format was announced and predicted that there weren't enough 7:00–9:00 A.M. watchers in the country for two programs. Paar proved them wrong. Within six months he grew a network of nearly sixty stations reaching all the way to the Rocky Mountains and to an audience of four million families.

His "cute little Presbyterian face" (as he once described it) and outspoken attitudes and oddball stunts attracted over two thousand fan letters a week, mostly pro-Paar. Home audiences began watching the show and not just listening to it —as they often did to the opposing *Today Show*—because most of Paar's humor was visual. He wore bare feet on camera to complement his new blue suit. He played ping-pong in the rafters of the studio. His cast, made up of Pupi Campo, a singer named Betty Clooney, pianist and old Army buddy Jose Melis, and announcer Hank Simms often joined him in satires of television shows, of quiz programs, of serious discussion forums. His bizarre humor came out in waspish asides about cast members, about the *Today Show* ("Don't watch it") and even his skits. In one of them, he was a boy strangler whose mother gave him a Lucrezia Borgia poison kit as a loving birthday gift.

NBC's Chairman of the Board, Robert Sarnoff, decided to break the bad news-good news himself.

"The *America After Dark* version of our *Tonight Show* was a shambles. Sponsors were shunning the program. Some stations were deserting from the NBC late night line-up in favor of old Hollywood movies. We were under heavy pressure to give up late night live programming. After much soul searching we staked everything on an amiable young man named Jack Paar."

Dick Linkroum then described the new *Tonight Show* as "a low-gear variety show with a permanent orchestra, no scenery, rising young musicians, offbeat guests and interviewees. . . . We'll wing it," he continued. "It'll be off the cuff, a free-for-all. It will be quite different from Allen's *Tonight*."

Paar had his own opinions about the program. He had been brooding about informal talk-type shows since his departure from CBS more than a year ago. He had come up with some new ideas for what was basically a new type of program. Paar wanted to add a panel to discuss everything from popular song lyrics to fashions and new books. He also made immediate plans to use old chums from the CBS show including a famous party-giver of the time, Elsa Maxwell, a cigar-smoking British comedienne named Hermione Gingold, folk singer Burl Ives, author and playwright Jean Kerr, and anybody who could talk—amusingly, interestingly, even weirdly.

"My thought," Paar said, "is to let everybody talk about whatever they want, with certain provisions of good taste, of course—crackpot diets, the unhealthiness of wearing underwear. We'd have to be ready to cut them off—maybe fast. . . ."

In many cases nobody cut Jack Paar off fast enough.

Very early, he forecast what might lie ahead when he said the Jack Paar version of the *Tonight Show* would be nothing like the Steve Allen version. He criticized Allen for stealing jokes and material from him, said that Allen was the greatest living non-authority on comedy. To top it off, he added that payola had been a way of life on the previous *Tonight Show*.

Another time, having luncheon with an NBC executive, he said, "I've always thought of you as Steve Allen's friend. Tell me, is Allen as rotten as he's supposed to be?"

"No, but you are," answered the NBC executive. He was taken off the show.

Outbursts like this led one reviewer to write that Paar was the only bull with his own china shop. Someone else topped that by suggesting that they erect a statue of Paar with a fig leaf over its mouth. During his five years with *Tonight*, Paar managed to pick fights with NBC censors, Ed Sullivan, the United States Senate, Walter Winchell, Jimmy Hoffa, pro-Castro Cubans, columnists Dorothy Kilgallen, Jack O'Brien, Jack Gould, Lee Mortimer and Irv Kupcinet, and a dozen newspapers and magazines. He had also fought with William S. Paley, CBS board chairman, a

Variety editor, Fred Allen, Pupi Campo and just about everybody who had worked with or for him.

Tonight—starring Jack Paar went on the air at eleven-fifteen the night of July 29, 1957. That first week, it had Paar, it had Melis, announcer Hugh Downs, a wacky blonde named Dody Goodman, a model named Tedi Thurman ("the weather girl") and a sign behind Paar which changed nightly. One night it said, "Stop looking at the blackboard." Another night it said, "No U Turn in the Tunnel." That time period —previously occupied by *Tonight! America After Dark*—was now down to 135th in a list of 135 rated shows. It had less than a 1 rating.

Paar had only sixty-two stations when he started and there were two surviving sponsors. NBC had small hope that the relatively unknown Jack Paar could "talk" them out of their problems.

After a few nights of watching the new format, one critic sat down at his typewriter and tapped out, "The *Tonight Show* consists of people sitting around trying to change the subject."

Two months later, a critic on the Norfolk *Virginian Pilot* wrote, "Back in the days when Steve Allen was presiding over the late-hour television on NBC, my cup ran over. I wish I could say the same for the current edition of *Tonight!*

"While—to me—Jack Paar is hilariously funny at times, he simply does not have enough material at hand to fill a 90 minute spot, five nights per week." He added toward the end of his review, "If 'Steverino' hadn't got me in the habit of sitting up for this one, I probably wouldn't bother to watch it now."

Even Paar was being offhand about the show at this point. One night he commented, "It's the kind of show that if you miss it, you don't feel bad."

Between the opening night and that crack, however, Paar and his talent coordinators and writers had been trying anything that made a noise. They had on authors, photographers, singers, dancers and actors. Carol Burnett appeared one night and sang, "I Made a Fool of Myself over John Foster Dulles." The show started a feature called "It's All Relative" which used relatives of famous people on the show while the panel tried to guess the famous person. International party-giver Elsa Maxwell came on with opinions and attitudes. Paar's head writer, Jack Douglas, began to sit and trade jokes with Jack. Peter Ustinov began his long career of telling stories on talk shows. Even Shelley Berman came on and did a standup act sitting down. A young singer named Betty Johnson had been added to sing and to sit on the panel. Paar's producers also threw in a "What Is It" guessing game in which Paar held up odd-looking objects and then explained what they were. Ideas were so short, they even programmed a "Magic Time" and let Paar do magic tricks that didn't work.

Much of the program didn't either.

In desperation, Paar even reached back to the Allen show for studio-audience participation and began to interview people in the theatre.

Behind the cameras, Paar called the audience "the ribbon counter people" and his skin crawled at the idea of mixing with them. He didn't like to shake hands. He didn't like strangers. One of his writers even commented that Paar didn't like somebody else's shadow to fall on him.

One night, in a wicked mood, Paar decided to ding an old Steve Allen regular, Miss Miller, who was now in his audience every night. He knew that she liked the prizes that had been given her through the years and must have thought that was the main reason for her constant attendance.

"Tell me," he said, chuckling, "why exactly is it you're here?"

The small, gray-faced woman thought for a moment seriously, then said softly, "Because I'm lonely."

Paar retreated to the stage.

One night the writers planted Cary Grant in the audience

as a gag. Paar completely overlooked him, interviewed the woman sitting next to the motion picture star.

Another time he picked out a cherubic young boy and patted him on the head and began to interview him. The boy waded patiently through Paar's questions, then said, "Mr. Paar, Mr. Paar."

"Yes, what is it? Something you want to know?"

"Yes, Mr. Paar. Do you wear a toupee?"

Paar backed out of the audience red-faced and red-scalped under the toupee.

Suddenly, *Tonight* and Paar began to make news. On the night of October 10, Jack Paar introduced a seventeen-year-old singer from Pennsylvania named Trish Dwelley. He said that earlier that day he and other staffers had auditioned Trish and that everybody had been so excited about her talent they had asked her to be on that night as their new discovery. Paar went on to explain that there hadn't been time to costume her so she would sing in the plain simple sweater and skirt she had worn to the audition. Trish sang three numbers and an instant star was born. Newspapers picked up her "Cinderella" story and clapped Paar on the back for discovering her. Decca Records offered her a contract. Motion picture studios offered her screen tests. She was signed as a regular member of the cast for the *Tonight Show*.

A few days later someone yelled fraud. It turned out that Trish Dwelley was a professional, that she had sung with a group called the Dreamweavers, that she had been on the *Perry Como Show* and other television programs as a member of that group.

Faced with the exposé, Paar verbally relieved himself on the program, for the first time in what was to become a series of self-confessions and flagellations for the next five years. Paar admitted that he had been naïve, that he hadn't asked Trish what professional experience she had so Trish hadn't really lied to him.

"Okay," he ended his commentary, "I'm naïve—I thought I had made a discovery. Well, I still think I have made a discovery!" He indicated they would keep her on the show. However, two weeks later she was gone and the reason given was, "Her costumes and arrangements were too expensive for the program."

By early December, the seventy-four-year-old Elsa Maxwell was a Tuesday night regular. She was an outspoken woman who was once described by Paar this way: "If you use Elsa you have to push her all together, then squeeze her out all at once. You don't drop her, you have to plop her."

Sometimes Maxwell's comments plopped all over Paar and the *Tonight Show*. One night she was indignant about a letter she had received. The letter said that rock singer Elvis Presley had autographed the chests of eight teen-age girls. Maxwell took a deep breath, then pronounced Presley "horribly dreadful" and "a menace to our country."

British comedienne Hermione Gingold, another show regular, commented, "I don't see why she's so upset. You could write a three-act play on her bosom."

For months, Maxwell attacked the personalities and peculiarities of "Fatso" Farouk, then King of Egypt plus billionaire J. Paul Getty and movie starlet Jayne Mansfield without getting much reaction. One night, however, she made big news when she turned her venom against newspaper columnist Walter Winchell. She had been cued into her accusation when Paar commented that Winchell was "after him."

Elsa was enraged. "He's never voted and never registered! Is that a good patriotic American or not? He is phonier than we are, Jack!"

Encouraged, Paar joined in. He said that Winchell's "high, hysterical voice" resulted from wearing "too tight underwear" and that Winchell would like a show similar to *Tonight* but couldn't handle it, in fact, had flopped on four previous shows.

Winchell slapped back. He called Maxwell fat and sloppy

and smelly. He claimed that her accusations had endangered the Damon Runyon Cancer Fund, a charity which Winchell had founded. He said people had stopped donating because of Maxwell's remarks and he was planning to make up for it by suing all twelve of Paar's sponsors for two million dollars each. He demanded a retraction from Paar and said he would take Maxwell into court.

Winchell sent along a photograph of him entering a voting booth in New York.

The feud bloomed. Winchell wrote that Paar was trying to make boredom entertaining. Elsa snapped back that Winchell was a fading TV star while the American public *loved* Elsa. Paar, meanwhile, was pressured by NBC management and he went on the show one night to present the Winchell voting picture to his viewers. He said he was happy to set the record straight, but he couldn't resist adding that Winchell had once carried a gossipy item about the Paars. "Friends of the Jack Paars are worrying . . ." was all it said. That was on April 22.

Elsa Maxwell was last seen on the Jack Paar *Tonight Show* one week later.

This was the second abrupt disappearance of a cast member within the first season of the show. About six weeks before Maxwell left the program, the malaprop-ridden blonde ex-dancer Dody Goodman had been let go. Dody Goodman was once described as someone you avoid at the laundromat. She had been a dancer in the Broadway shows *High Button Shoes* and *Wonderful Town*. She had auditioned as a guest dancer for the show but her interview had gone so strangely that Paar at one point asked if she was for real.

"A little," she answered.

She had joined the show in the first week and she helped Paar with skits, did a dumb-blonde act and, in general, imitated Dagmar, the mammary-laden blonde who had been on *Broadway Open House*. One night Dody talked about her dog. Paar asked what kind it was. She spelled M-u-t-t. "I didn't want to insult him in case he's watching." That was the type of humor Paar had assigned to her.

Sometimes the conversations between Paar and Goodman became tense, shrill, biting. One night, commenting on a Goodman remark, Paar said, "Give them enough rope . . ."

Ad-libbing, Goodman answered, "And they'll skip."

"Go ahead," Paar snapped back. "This end's untied."

Soon she was gone.

A lot of them came and a lot of them went.

Tedi Thurman, the sexy weather girl, lasted three and a half months.

Bil and Cora Baird's puppets came on to great applause, were announced as weekly regulars, were gone within half a year.

Singer Betty Johnson lasted eight months.

Others came and went, came and went.

The producers, the writers, and later the talent coordinators searched through newspapers, magazines, newsreels, motion pictures, fan magazines and other radio and television shows for "characters." It wasn't enough to be interesting, amusing, informed or entertaining. The talent search was on for what one coordinator called "nuts, but well-known nuts." Sometimes they went too far. "No, I do *not* want the man with the longest toenail in the world," Paar turned down one opportunity.

One night, while reminiscing about early radio days, Paar asked guest Fran Allison (of *Kukla, Fran and Ollie*) what had ever happened to Cliff Arquette. Arquette had been a continuing character on the old *Fibber McGee and Molly* radio show, had been the one who said, "Pretty funny, Bub, but that ain't the way I heard it."

The next day a telegram arrived from Arquette which said, "Have old man suit. Will travel." Paar sent for him and put him on the show. For two nights he played himself and demonstrated why he was no longer in show business. The third night he did Charley Weaver, the baggy-pantsed, rustic comic from "Mount Idy" who read "letters from my mother." From that appearance on, Arquette was a steady guest on the program. So successful was he that eventually he had his own program on the ABC network, a best-selling book, a hit record album of letters, a successful Civil War Museum in his home town of Gettysburg, Pennsylvania, and he had a beer mug, a popsicle and a cologne set named after him.

There is a famous tavern-saloon-bar across the street from NBC's New York headquarters. It is called Hurley's. Arquette spent so much time in there before and after shows they almost renamed that bar after him too. He once combined his interest in Civil War things with his interest in liquor and made up a song called "The Bottle Hymn of the Republic."

Paar also found a petite French singer named Geneviève whose hair style and English language were both shaggy at the edges. Geneviève had appeared on the old Steve Allen *Tonight Show* but more as a singer than a talker. On the Paar version, she was used as what the writers call a "cute." They gave her fractured-English lines. One night she was talking about New York and said that she had "crossed Greta Garbo on the street." Another time she was talking about her father coming to visit her in New York. "He will take a fly from Paris," she informed the audience. Paar began giving her news items to read. One night he gave her the baseball scores. She obediently read off the runs, hits and when she got to the third column referred to errors as *faux pas*.

Paar's head writer, Jack Douglas, often appeared and delivered some material originally intended for Paar. When Douglas married a tiny Japanese girl named Reiko, his act became a double and Reiko came out with lines strongly resembling Geneviève's humor.

Accents dripped all over the show.

Zsa Zsa Gabor appeared again and again, with lines like "European men are better lovers than American men because of European women," and "They taught me in school that money wasn't everything. That's why Mama made me quit school."

Hermione Gingold came on with her heavy British accent and said things like "Else Maxwell is just another pretty face."

A television time salesman named Pat Harrington, Jr., appeared as an Italian golf pro named Guido Panzini. His comedy was built around golf. "In the African Open, I shot 77—and 4 Mau Mau," he once cracked.

A press agent named Jim Moran, who had broken into talk shows with many appearances on Steve Allen's *Tonight*, began to appear and retell the stories of how he found the needle in the haystack and sold a refrigerator to an Eskimo.

A Hollywood-based actor named Hans Conried dropped in from time to time and told "theatuh" stories in a rolling Shakespearean tone.

Peggy Cass, a folk actress and singer, began to come on the show and tell down-home stories.

Mary Margaret McBride, a sociologist type, sat on the panel for a while and commented on things sociological.

A very funny man named Alexander King, who billed himself as a writer and observer of the scene, almost took over the Paar show with his stories and anecdotes.

The house rule became funny stories. If a person had ten of them, a guest appearance could be arranged even if the guest's expertise was cancer research.

The most controversial and over-all funniest guest was a classical pianist and professional hypochondriac from Beverly Hills, California, named Oscar Levant. Levant shuffled, snuffled, winced, cringed, whined, coughed, shuddered, trembled and clutched his way through each appearance. He continually protested that he was a very ill man and should be home in bed. He grabbed his heart from time to time "to make sure it was still beating." He had an acid-tipped arrow for many subjects. Talking about his career, he said, "Everything I touch turns to pennies." He said, "Zsa Zsa has discovered the secret of perpetual middle age." He said he never watched the Dinah Shore television show because he was a diabetic. Levant once suggested that Elizabeth Taylor be awarded the "Other Woman of the Year Award." He called ballet "fairies' baseball." He said a newsreel was a series of catastrophes ending with a fashion show. He confessed that he was once thrown out of a mental hospital for depressing the other patients. And reporting on his command perform- ance and dinner at the White House, he commented, "Now I suppose we'll have to have the Trumans over to our place." Somebody said, if Levant didn't exist, you couldn't make him up.

Paar and Levant whipped through thirty years of Oscar's lines as though the comments had just been snapped out of the air.

That was one type of humor. Paar also had the professional comics on to do their material and to visit for a while. He presented everyone from Mike Nichols and Elaine May to Jack Benny, who admitted on the show that he was then sixty-six. Paar avoided some comics. He once said, "I am not interested in comedians named Joey or Jackie." Later, when Henny Youngman (a Joey-Jackie type comic) said Paar had a great show, Paar cried.

Other humor happened spontaneously.

One night when he was slated to do a Bufferin commer- cial, Paar couldn't get the tablets out of the small bottle. In trying to get the cotton out of the bottle mouth, he poured water into it, then turned it over. About thirty minutes later the bottle exploded and blew melted aspirin all over Paar, the guests and part of the audience. "First time Bufferin's ever created a headache," someone said.

One night Paar was trying to do a Norelco electric razor commercial, but Zsa Zsa wouldn't be still.

"Be careful, be careful," she repeated over and over.

"I am being careful," answered Paar.

"It'll cut you," Zsa Zsa screamed.

"It won't cut anything!" Paar snapped back and then gulped, turned white and smiled weakly.

Another time the entire cast and crew of the show turned white. It was the night a singer named Danny Scholl collapsed during the show. He was moved to the hospital, paralyzed, and later died there.

Paar booked authors like Rona Jaffe, war heroes like Colonel "Pappy" Boyington (who made disparaging remarks about his service career), comedians like Jonathan Winters, anthropologists like Ashley Montagu, who said that American men had breast fixations because their mothers didn't let them breast-feed enough, a pickpocket who lifted Paar's belt and wrist watch, a wrestler named Killer Kowalski and forty different sponsors ranging from Minipoo shampoo to Corega Denture Fastener.

By late 1958, mixing this all together, along with his steady guests, the well-known kooks and his controversial comments, Paar's *Tonight Show* grew to a five-million nightly audience tuned in to 115 stations. In its second year the show had a higher rating than the very successful Steve Allen *Tonight Show*. The main reason for this was the dramatic increase in television set ownership and in the number of cities serviced with television and late night shows.

Paar's salary was now up to $2750 a week plus a percentage of the commercials and his new contract was written through 1960. It guaranteed him six weeks of vacation with pay. It also gave him many Mondays off in addition to the every Friday vacations. The Friday shows had become kinescoped repeats.

Substituting for him when he was ill, tired or away were a bright young California comedian named Johnny Carson and a club comic named Joey Bishop.

By now, Paar was beginning to recognize his reach and impact. He had fired Dick Linkroum, the NBC producer who fought so long and hard to get him the *Tonight Show* job. He ran the program with a heavy hand, arbitrarily throwing out writer material, sometimes throwing out the writers, canceling guests at the last minute because he didn't like them, complaining to the world that he was surrounded by incompetents and hacks.

One time he said, "On the air all I do is hold back. If I gave too much of myself on the show, it would be too much for the cable."

On one other occasion, when people were telling him how good his guests were, he said, "I thought *me* was pretty good too."

He stalked the stage like a hunted man, refused to sign autograph books or talk to strangers or join the crew at meals or after the show.

"The next time someone slaps me on the back it could have a knife in it," he said suspiciously.

One of the writers, talking about him one night, said, "He's a catalyst."

"The catalyst that swallowed the canary," another popped back.

Another writer commented, "As a guy who loves his work and hates liquor, loves his family and hates night clubs, loves his suburban home and hates late hours, Jack Paar is proof positive that clean living will not guarantee a man tranquillity."

From the time Paar took on the *Tonight Show* until he left it, neither the program nor Paar was ever tranquil.

Much of Jack Paar's prior life had not been tranquil either.

He was born in Canton, Ohio, in 1918, one of four children of Howard and Lillian Paar. He had a standard, middle-class childhood, with standard middle-class ambitions. His parents wanted him to be a minister, but he wanted to be a wrestler. He stuttered badly as a child and he read somewhere that the Greek orator Demosthenes had filled his mouth with pebbles and made speeches to the sea. Having no nearby sea near Canton, he made do with his living room and with buttons from his mother's sewing basket.

When he was sixteen, the Paars moved to Jackson, Michigan. Here Jack Paar got his first job on radio. He had been walking down the street when he noticed a man-on-the-street reporter interviewing several citizens of Jackson. Paar wormed his way into the group, then up to the microphone and once he started talking could hardly be chased away. His personal talkathon led to a part-time job at a local station for three dollars a week. At eighteen, he left home and hopped around the country from radio station to radio station—in Indianapolis, Youngstown, Cleveland, Pittsburgh, Buffalo. Along the way he married the same girl twice and divorced her twice.

In 1942 he was called into the Army and assigned to the 28th Special Service Company as part of an entertainment troupe. He was given a microphone but no instructions on its care and use or on the care and use of officers either. He decided that what he and the other enlisted men had in common was resentment of the war and the way the officers lived. He used both to create a type of service comedy. On a ship going overseas, Paar grabbed the mike one day and made an announcement. He said, "I've been asked to tell you that there was a Japanese submarine in the vicinity, but unfortunately the Navy gun crews have driven it off. I say unfortunately because the Japanese submarine was trying to bring us food."

In wartime, on a troop ship, the listeners laughed until they fell off their barracks bags.

He began to pepper the brass. On a South Pacific island tour, he took on a Navy Commodore and a nurse who arrived late for the show.

"We were going to have six lovely girls do the dance of the virgins," cracked Paar, "but they broke their contracts by being with the Commodore." He also said, "You'd think one man and a broad wouldn't hold up five thousand enlisted men." After the show he was arrested and held for court-martial. The Army rescued him by promising the Navy they would ship him to Okinawa.

A war correspondent named Sidney Carroll was intrigued by the little-known Army entertainment units. He had heard about Paar's troupe at a USO show. "You think these guys are funny," said one mud-smeared G.I. to Carroll about two top-notch Hollywood comedians on a USO show, "you should see Jack Paar." Carroll did and then wrote an article for *Esquire* magazine about Paar and the G.I. entertainers.

"They went on month after month, untouted, unheralded, like the foot-slogging infantry itself, doing a job that had to be done, making men laugh in some of the most laughproof places in the world," he wrote.

He added, "Paar is funny and Paar is likable and it's impossible to get mad at him. I know why he became a demigod among the men he entertained in the Pacific."

Paar's publicity got back to the States before he did, and when he was discharged he had a job to go to at RKO motion picture studios. Not much came of it. As Paar once observed, "They decided I looked like a new Alan Ladd. Unfortunately there was plenty of mileage left in the *old* Alan Ladd."

Shortly after one "unforgettable" experience playing opposite an "unforgettable" starlet named Marilyn Monroe in an "unforgettable" film named *Love Nest*, Paar went back to radio. He was hired to replace Jack Benny for the summer. He was a success at once and when fall came he was put on ABC with his own show sponsored by the American Tobacco Company. Paar immediately began "attacking the officers." He fought with everyone, fired writers by the pair, became embittered toward a *Daily Variety* columnist named Jack Hellman and once put a nameplate "Hellman" on a monkey and paraded it through Hollywood.

The show went off at Christmas.

Paar began to fill in for anyone who was ill, on vacation or too drunk to go on. He substituted for Eddie Cantor, for Arthur Godfrey, for Ed Sullivan.

Radio and television columnist John Crosby of the New York *Herald Tribune* wrote, "I have learned to tell the seasons by Jack Paar. When Paar appears it is time to lay away the winter clothes in mothballs and get out the tennis racket."

He next did a quiz show called *Up to Paar* which the critics said definitely was not, a CBS radio show called *Bank on the Stars,* on which viewers did not bank, and finally he replaced Walter Cronkite on the *Morning Show.* Although that did not last, he developed a reputation as a man who could fill time inexpensively and entertainingly. NBC found him ideal to head the salvage operation on the *Tonight Show.* They had little indication that Paar would create five of the most controversial broadcasting years in television history.

On February 3, 1959, Paar did his first Cuban program. It was a twenty-two-minute special film report on *The Background of a Revolution.* It had been put together by Paar and author Jim Bishop during a stay in Havana. The film showed the Cuban people's reactions to the revolution then going on. Paar and Bishop interviewed a taxi driver who had joined Fidel Castro's men after being beaten by Batista's troops. The film showed a tank made from an International Harvester tractor. There was an interview with a Staten Island youth who had joined Castro's army. There were film shots of Batista's glorious homes contrasted to films of a camp where political prisoners were being held.

This program did not make Batista sympathizers in the United States too happy with Paar. The show began to receive threatening mail and obscene phone calls.

Two months later the program was interrupted with a Cuban bomb scare.

Despite it, Paar remained interested in Cuba and Castro. (He once cracked it was because Castro talked longer than he did.) On January 27, 1960, he began to talk about Castro's new leadership for Cuba. Paar said the press was presenting incorrect facts about Cuba; that Castro was loved by his people, that Castro had been needled by Americans from the very beginning and that Americans had been unfair to him.

Steve Allen and Jonathan Winters

Jack Paar with Eddie Fisher and Elizabeth Taylor

John Lennon and Paul McCartney
with Joe Garagiola and Ed McMahon

Paar with Robert Kennedy

V.P. Spiro Agnew with Johnny Carson

Paar and Richard M. Nixon

Left: Senator Hubert H. Humphrey and Johnny Carson

Bottom left: Sammy Davis, Jr., Robert Kennedy

Below: Jack Paar, Errol Flynn and Geneviève

Paar and JFK

At one point, Paar was interrupted by an audience member who questioned his attitudes. Paar attacked the man for not being sympathetic to Castro.

Paar ran into other problems with the open-mouth format of his program. On January 12, 1960, he showed a two-minute, forty-second film of the Cape Florida section of Key Biscayne, near Miami. Paar said this was the area where he had put money down on a lot. He described it as a glorious place to live—lush, beautiful, serene.

The United States House of Representatives Special Subcommittee on Legislative Oversight met in hurried session, questioned whether the film was a commercial, whether there had been a paid sponsor, and whether Paar was guilty of payola. Paar denied taking anything from the real estate firm, which had been identified on the film.

About a year later Paar ran into the same problem when an actor named Lou Holtz "accidentally" mentioned a stock that was then selling for ten dollars a share. "It'll be up to a hundred in ten years," said Holtz. The Securities Exchange Commission investigated, scolded, threatened NBC and Paar with action but nothing came of it. The stock did go up.

From the beginning, Paar attracted newsmakers. On July 22, 1959, the chief counsel for the Senate Select Committee Investigating Improper Practices in Labor or Management Fields appeared on the program. His name was Robert Kennedy. He talked about organized crime infiltrating labor unions. He talked about the danger of men like Johnny Dioguardi, Tony "Ducks" Corrallo and Jimmy Hoffa getting into honest unions and making them branches of organized crime. He said some hard, tough things about Jimmy Hoffa, provisional president of the Teamsters Union, and he challenged Hoffa to come and see him.

Paar made news—with Debbie Reynolds—two months later when they both giggled and went behind his desk, while she partially undressed him.

A month after that, Paar had the Canadian doctor Tom

Dooley on the program. Dooley had returned to the United States from his hospital in Asia to try to raise funds and equipment for the hospital. His second reason for coming back was to have an operation for cancer. Paar saluted the brave doctor, asked the public to help. Among other offerings, a jeep was donated for his work in the jungle.

Within a period of two months, Paar had fights with two celebrities. The first happened on December 1, 1960, when motion picture actor Mickey Rooney was a guest on the show. Paar noticed that Rooney listed to starboard in his chair, answered questions with a lopsided grin, stared blankly off into space, and now and then would appear to be asleep. Paar decided that Rooney was drunk and thought that asking him questions might bring him around. When that approach didn't work, Paar made some comment about Rooney's drinking.

"Listen, I'm not a fan of yours, you know," said Rooney. "I don't care to watch your show."

"Would you care to leave?" Paar answered, ushering him off the air.

The next morning, thinking it over, Rooney called Paar at his hotel in Hollywood and threatened to come over and punch him in the nose. Paar knew that Rooney was small but that he had been known to travel with professional football players as bodyguards. When Rooney arrived at the hotel, he was attended by several large friends. Paar decided the only way to keep peace was to get Rooney away from the muscle. He invited Mickey into the room, explained why he had acted that way and apologized for any damage to Mickey's reputation. Mickey took the remarks graciously, said it was certainly his fault and it was nice of Paar to understand. They shook hands on their renewed friendship and Paar offered Rooney a drink before he realized that was what had started the entire problem.

In early February, Paar pulled a soapbox up to his microphone and began to dissect a New York columnist named

Dorothy Kilgallen. Kilgallen, in one of her columns, had implied that Paar was a Communist because of his attitudes toward Cuba and Castro. Paar began to insult Kilgallen, even said that she had no right to make her column-carried remark about Premier Khrushchev's wife having no ankles, since she, Kilgallen, had no chin.

He kept it up. The next night he bitterly attacked Kilgallen for the way she was covering the current murder trial of Dr. Bernard Finch in California. He attacked her professionally and personally.

"Jesus, is he strung out these days. Something's going to blow," one of his crew commented.

Eight days later, it did.

Although Paar said he never approved off-color stories on the air, critics noticed that a lot of material on his show had azure or cobalt tints around the edges. On the February 10, 1960 show Paar had included a story which he considered cute and not smutty. Bathroom jokes were funny to Paar, bedroom jokes were forbidden.

The network censors, however, didn't consider his story cute, considered it dirty, and snipped the entire story from the tape without telling him about it. When Paar watched the show from his home that night, there was a four-minute hole in the program he thought he had done. This is the story they had cut out:

An English lady, while visiting in Switzerland, was looking for a room, and she asked the schoolmaster if he could recommend any to her. He took her to see several rooms, and when everything was settled, the lady returned to her home to make the final preparations to move. When she arrived home, the thought suddenly occurred to her that she had not seen a W.C. (water closet) around the place. So she immediately wrote a note to the schoolmaster asking him if there was a W.C. around. The schoolmaster was a very poor student of English, so he asked the parish priest if he could help in the matter. Together they tried to discover the meaning of the letters W.C. and the only solution they could find for the letters was a Wayside Chapel. The schoolmaster then wrote to the English lady the following note:

Dear Madam:

I take great pleasure in informing you that the W.C. is situated nine miles from the house you occupy, in the center of a beautiful grove of pine trees surrounded by lovely grounds.

It is capable of holding 229 people and it is open on Sunday and Thursday only. As there are a great number of people and they are expected during the summer months, I would suggest that you come early: although there is plenty of standing room as a rule.

You will no doubt be glad to hear that a good number of people bring their lunch and make a day of it. While others who can afford to go by car arrive just in time. I would especially recommend that your ladyship go on Thursday when there is a musical accompaniment.

It may interest you to know that my daughter was married in the W.C. and it was there that she met her husband. I can remember the rush there was for seats. There were ten people to a seat ordinarily occupied by one. It was wonderful to see the expression on their faces.

The newest attraction is a bell donated by a wealthy resident of the district. It rings every time a person enters. A bazaar is to be held to provide plush seats for all the people, since they feel it is a long-felt need. My wife is rather delicate, so she can't attend regularly.

I shall be delighted to reserve the best seat for you if you wish, where you will be seen by all. For the children, there is a special time and place so that they will not disturb the elders. Hoping to have been of service to you, I remain,

Sincerely,
The Schoolmaster

Although it was a very funny joke, nobody at NBC was laughing.

Jack Paar walked off his show.

At 11:41 P.M.—New York network time—on February 11, 1960, NBC's watchman of the very late, very profitable hours walked off his job.

Jack Paar had gone through the first twenty minutes of the show in a routine manner but then he suddenly began talking about his problem with the network. He told the audience that NBC had cut a water-closet joke out of his previous night's show without talking to him and that NBC made him look like a little boy who needed reprimanding. He'd been up for thirty hours wrestling with his conscience, he said, and . . .

"I've made a decision about what I'm going to do. And only one person knows about this—it's Hugh Downs. My wife doesn't know about it, but I'll be home in time and I'll tell her." The program was taped by 10:00 P.M., which gave Paar time to get home before it was aired at eleven-fifteen. "I'm leaving the *Tonight Show*."

Choked with emotion, he drank a cup of water, then continued, "There must be a better way to making a living than this. There's a way of entertaining people without being constantly involved in some form of controversy which is on me all the time.

"It's rough on my wife and child, and I don't need it. . . .

"I took over a show with 60 stations, there's now 158, the show is sold out, it's the highest, I think, producer for this network, and I believe I was let down by this network at a time when I could have used their help."

He turned to the audience and said, "You have been peachy to me always."

He walked across the stage and shook hands with Hugh Downs, said a soft good-by, walked off the stage and out of the studio.

In the studio the audience sat stunned for a moment, then buzzed excitedly, then stood and cheered and clapped for almost a minute.

At homes all over the country, viewers said, "Jeezus, did you hear that?" or "Hey, honey, c'mere. Paar just quit," or "Hey, turn the TV on, Myrtle just called and said something's going on at the *Tonight Show*."

When the audience quieted down, Hugh Downs shook his head sadly and said, "Jack frequently does things he regrets. But I'd like to think this is not final and that he will be back."

Even though he was now running the show, Downs stayed in his regular seat and left Paar's chair unoccupied. That evening's guests were comedians Shelley Berman and Orson Bean. Bolstering each other, they agreed that NBC had been out of line, yes, that's it, out of line, for censoring Paar, especially, yes, especially, without telling Paar about it. Downs rode the fence, said that he didn't believe the story was a proper one for television, but that he certainly didn't believe in censorship and that under the circumstances Paar's walkoff was understandable.

PAAR FIRES NETWORK! bannered one Los Angeles newspaper.

NBC LIMPS AFTER PAAR WALKS, cracked a Hollywood trade sheet.

MILLIONS WATCH PAAR QUIT! headlined a New York daily.

Jack Gould of the New York *Times* wrote, "Mr. Paar is not the traditional trouper; he is a creation of television. If he began as a light humorist, his forte on his own show has been an outspokenness that has not alienated viewers weary of nice nellyism and self-appointed sacred cows who can dish out criticism but cannot take it."

Telephones rang. Thousands of viewers kept those protesting letters and postcards coming. More radio and television news time and more newspaper and magazine space was devoted to the Paar pique than to any event of the moment.

Illinois Governor Adlai Stevenson, in a speech to the Society of Newspaper Editors in Washington, D.C., commented that he had made a study of American newspapers for one week. The Russians and Mikoyan were trying to take over Cuba. The Russians and Khrushchev were trying to take over India. The French had developed and tested their own atomic bomb. The United States was becoming a second-rate military power, according to our generals. But the big story in most newspapers, Stevenson smiled, was about a television talk show host who had quit his job.

Opinions collided in the halls at 30 Rockefeller Plaza.

"Let him go. I can get Joey or Jerry or Frankie to take over the show," said one executive, running one way with a copy of the William Morris talent agency roster in his hand.

"Find Paar, get him back!" yelled another executive, running the other way. "Say anything, pay anything, but find him!"

Paar was in Hong Kong where one wag said he had gone to see if he had a Chinaman's chance of getting his show back.

John Crosby wrote a column called "The Fall of Jack Paar." In it, Crosby said that Jack was washed up in television and that he couldn't get his job back even if he wanted it back. That column and Paar's changeable mind brought him back to NBC.

"When I walked off, I said there must be a better way of making a living," Paar commented on his return March 7 —roughly five weeks after he had left. "Well, I've looked, and there isn't. Be it ever so humble, there is no place like Radio City.

"Leaving the show," he continued, "was a childish and perhaps emotional thing. I have been guilty of such action in the past and will perhaps be again. I'm totally unable to hide what I feel. It is not an asset in show business. But I shall do the best I can to amuse and entertain you and let other people speak freely, as I have in the past. Any who are maligned will find this show a place to come and tell their story. There will be a rock in every snowball and I plan to continue exactly what I started out to do. I hope you will find it interesting."

Without taking a breath, Paar then made some remarks about Walter Winchell. He called him a silly old man, commented on his virility. Later, playing the good guy, he agreed to NBC's request to cut seven seconds out of the tape in order to keep Winchell's attorney from filing more lawsuits against NBC.

Strengthened by his hearty welcome home from entertainers, from NBC, from the letter- and postcard-writing public, Paar began attracting controversies like he attracted sponsors. One of his writers, Walter Kempley, who later went on to produce the *Merv Griffin Show*, said, "For the first couple of years, things happened to Paar. After his walkout, however, Paar happened to things. The network realized that Paar was the type who would always be in trouble and that trouble

attracted viewers and viewers attracted ratings and advertisers."

The night after he returned, Paar had Robert Kennedy
on the show. This was the night Kennedy, now chief
counsel of the Senate Labor-Management Relations Committee, warned the public that organized crime was moving
into the labor unions. He named names, including Teamster
boss James Hoffa. This was the beginning of Kennedy's drive
to expose Hoffa, one that was to end with Hoffa filing a two-
and-a-half-million-dollar lawsuit against Kennedy and against
Paar. The lawsuit was later thrown out of court.

At the end of the month Paar decided to originate a week
of shows from London, England. The show was structured
as a London version of *Tonight* with a live audience at the
Wood Green Theatre of Associated Television. A set much
like the New York one was installed with a desk for Paar and
a chair and sofa for his panel guests. Even the films of New
York used at station-break times were replaced with similar
films of London. The English commercials were delivered in
American accents by Hugh Downs and Jack Paar. During the
week the show went quietly and easily. There were films of
the Paar family—Jack, his wife Miriam, and daughter Randy
arriving at Buckingham Palace to watch the changing of the
guard. Julie Andrews came on and sang "Wouldn't It Be
Loverly" from *My Fair Lady*. Peter Sellers appeared for some
dialogue and John Spencer Churchill showed up to play the
game "Mystery Relative."

Paar almost made it through the visit without an incident.
But not quite. During one show, someone asked him why
exactly he had flounced off his show.

"I didn't flounce," Paar snapped back. "That's only done at
BBC [the British Broadcasting Corporation] . . . or," he
thoughtfully added, "at your Admiralty Headquarters.

"An American walks off like this," he concluded, stood up,
did an exaggerated bowlegged cowboy walk and stalked from

the stage, leaving an aghast group and ten empty minutes behind him to fill.

Paar's compulsion to top others became part of his daily life.

One time he was comparing success with Ernie Kovacs. Kovacs had topped Paar in just about every department of conspicuous consumption.

Kovacs drove a Rolls-Royce, Paar had a lesser car. Kovacs lived in more than twenty rooms, Paar had smaller quarters. Paar made one last effort. "I pay a dollar apiece for my cigars," said Jack, blowing a mouthful of expensive Havana smoke toward Kovacs.

"I pay two dollars each for mine," smiled Kovacs indulgently, "and my cigar bill is over fifteen thousand dollars a year."

Stricken, Paar excused himself and headed directly to the famous tobacconist where Kovacs had his cigars made. There, a salesman soothed him, assured him that the store handled no cigars above a dollar each and that Mr. Kovacs must have been pulling Mr. Paar's leg.

There were two highlights on the show of June 16, 1960. Actress Anne Bancroft was suddenly overcome by the show, by the host, by its guests, and blurted out to Paar, "You know, I'm in love with you."

"But I'm married," protested the surprised host.

"That's all right," Miss Bancroft assured him, "I'll wait."

Miriam Paar wasn't at all surprised. Over the years, hundreds of letters and cards and telephone calls had warned her that Jack was "seeing" Geneviève on the side, that he was "involved" with Peggy Cass, that he "had a thing going" with Tedi Thurman, and that Zsa Zsa Gabor and Jack were "playing house" behind Miriam's back. Miriam catalogued all of the writers as misguided busybodies and pointed out that her husband's schedule hardly allowed him time for her, much less for any other ladies.

Later that evening, Paar introduced Massachusetts Senator John Kennedy as a guest. Political news was hot and speculation about who would be the Democratic nominee for President of the United States was on all front pages. With little introduction, Paar asked Kennedy if he would accept the vice-presidential nomination. No, Kennedy shot back, he was running for the presidency and if he was defeated he would stay in the Senate. Paar then took a microphone into the theatre and encouraged the audience to ask the young presidential aspirant any political questions that came to mind. Questions ranged from Russian weaponry to school integration. Kennedy handled the questions easily, swiftly and with seeming depth of knowledge and wisdom.

"JFK's appearance on the Paar show did a lot toward earning him the nomination," a political reporter wrote. "It should also have been a warning to Nixon that Kennedy could handle himself on camera and on his feet."

Nixon's turn came a couple of months later. Paar and the Vice-President were at the NBC studio in Washington. Paar asked Nixon about his experience in making important national decisions. Nixon said he was called upon for his opinions but the President had the ultimate decision to make. Nixon went on to criticize the Democratic platform for making promises to do more with less taxes. He pointed out that all programs cost money and money must come from the people.

Later in the show, the cameras cut to Mrs. Pat Nixon sitting in the audience with Randy Paar. They both came up on stage and sat on the panel. In Washington, the announcer, Stewart Finley, went into the audience and asked them to pose questions to the Vice-President. The cameras then cut away to New York, where Hugh Downs did the same thing in that audience. The show ended with Dick and Pat Nixon asking Paar for his autograph for their two daughters.

Such was Paar's fame at the time.

Paar became obviously partisan and pro-Nixon. To the audience, it was a forecast of the Nixon-Kennedy debates to come.

One night a month after the election, a woman in the studio audience began a quarrel with Paar about the popular vote system in the United States. Orson Bean, who was a guest on the show that night, said that Nixon would have carried four more states with one more vote in each.

The woman shouted, "No matter how he did it, Kennedy made it, so what are you talking about?"

Paar looked at her loftily and said, "Madam, at ease."

The lady shot back, "I ain't in the Army."

The fight continued, with Paar getting hotter and hotter, until a commercial break came and tempers calmed down.

Anger evidently remained in the air, however, because three nights later, when Hal March was substituting for Parr, George Jessel and Zsa Zsa Gabor began a battle that riddled the entire show. Jessel had started to tell a joke and Zsa Zsa interrupted him continually with disturbing comments. Finally, Jessel became angry. With a you-can't-talk-to-me-that-way attitude, Gabor threatened to walk off the show. She finally did and Hal March told Jessel to finish his joke while March went backstage, calmed her down and brought her back. From that time on, Gabor's appearances on talk shows increased, Jessel's went downhill.

Hardly a week went by without Paar stirring up something or somebody with a sometimes planned, sometimes unrehearsed remark.

One night he told his audience of millions that Randy had just received her first brassiere and he even mentioned the size.

Another night he backed comic Milt Kamin against a Wyoming senator. Kamin had used a routine which said there was no Wyoming, that it was drawn on the maps but didn't really exist. "Who has ever been to Wyoming?" Kamin asked. When the senator protested in the name of the Great Sovereign State of Wyoming, Paar laughed at the senator's objections too.

This wasn't the first time he had flaunted the authority of

the states. Once when guest Peggy Cass had received a writ from the state of Pennsylvania to appear there, Paar advised her—on the air—to ignore it.

One fight which Paar didn't start—but did not duck either —started in March of 1961. Ed Sullivan, the powerful master of ceremonies of his own very highly rated Sunday night variety show, advised all talent agencies that any performers who went on the Paar show for the $320 scale fee would be paid only $320 when they appeared on the Sullivan show. Sullivan protested that he had to pay as much as $5000 for the same act people did on the Paar show for several hundred and that, effective immediately, he was stopping the practice. The night that Paar told his audience about the dispute, the producers had lined up performers to come on the show and demonstrate their loyalty to Paar. On stage were Joey Bishop, Buddy Hackett and several show-business wives who were there to speak for their husbands without violating the current payment customs.

The next night, which was a regularly scheduled repeat show night, Paar telephoned the studio and talked about Ed Sullivan for six minutes and thirty-five seconds. Calling from his home in Bronxville—speaking directly to Sullivan and Sullivan's viewers—Paar said he had received a telegram from Ed asking if he could come on Paar's show to talk about the problem. Jack invited him to come ahead, any time. Paar rambled about Sullivan's action in starting this fight, in going to the newspapers with it, and in choking off income to actors and performers.

He said Sullivan was "more incoherent, more emotional and more nutty than I am."

He attacked the press for being partial to Sullivan, then said that he was willing to appear on Sullivan's show with or without an audience or Sullivan could come to the Paar show. He ended with, "Ed made his hammock—now let him try to stand up in it." The telephone call was cut into the taped show twice between eleven and eleven-forty-five that night.

On the following Monday night, Hugh Downs conducted the show for the first fifteen minutes, then introduced Paar as a guest. Paar began to talk about Ed Sullivan and stayed doggedly at his subject for a little less than an hour, interrupted only by commercials. He said that Sullivan was supposed to be on the show that night, had made many stipulations but still hadn't shown up. He said Sullivan wanted to use a TelePrompTer and read a prepared statement and not have a discussion.

Getting hot, Paar said, "Any idiot can read a TelePrompTer."

Then he added, "Ed Sullivan is a liar. That is libel. He must now sue and go to court. Under oath, I repeat, Ed Sullivan, you lied today."

Instead of suing, Sullivan said he would drop the whole matter. The New York *Times* described the entire confrontation as distasteful and said, "If the people of the Congo think we've gone back to the playpen, they can't be blamed."

Less than three weeks later, Paar was forced into an apology by Jack Benny, who was guesting on the Paar show.

Benny was about to play one of his violin solos when he suddenly said, "I'll play if you let me say something to you, and promise that you won't get angry. You've got to promise me."

Promised, Benny continued, "Sometimes I think you're absolutely nuts. You are really crazy. May I bring up the Ed Sullivan thing?"

"You did."

"Now," continued Jack Benny, "Sullivan happens to be one of my closest friends here in New York. And you know I got into radio through Ed Sullivan.

"Now, with all the trouble there is in the world today, why should you and he have fights? I mean, if you're going to be mad at someone be mad at Eichmann or somebody.

"I know you called him all those names . . . you did not mean one of them," Benny continued. "You just got yourself so nuts. You're so emotional that you scream and holler and cry, and as soon as you walk outside you forget about it."

Benny went on to point out that Sullivan didn't call Paar names, said that Paar was a sweet guy who went crazy, and then urged Paar to apologize.

"Now you tell everybody you're sorry. Now say it. Say you're sorry."

Paar shouted, "I'm sorry! I'm sorry!"

The audience roared their disapproval.

"I'm not angry," Paar said when the protests died down. "Boy, he'll never be on this show again, I'll tell you that."

Sportsmanship had never been one of Paar's claims to fame. One year, Paar and his show were nominated for an Emmy—the television industry's Oscar—in four different categories. It wasn't a matter of Paar winning an Emmy but a matter of how many he would win. Even the orchestra leader at the Awards said to Jack, "We've been rehearsing your theme song all afternoon."

One by one, the winners of the Emmy statues were called off and, one by one, the categories in which Paar had been nominated were won by others. When the fourth possible Emmy vanished in another direction, Paar turned to his wife and snapped, "I didn't want to come. And I'll never come to one of these affairs again."

Sometimes Paar's annoyance was justified.

One night, Johnny Carson and Steve Allen were together on a show originating in California and were talking about the nights when they had done the *Tonight Show*—Allen as a regular and Carson as a substitute.

"I know," one of them said, "let's call good old Jack and invite him in by phone on this reunion."

They placed the call on the air. The phone rang several times in Bronxville and finally it was answered by a sleepy-voiced Jack Paar.

"Hi, did we wake you?" someone asked brightly.

"Um-hm," Paar admitted.

"Did we wake Miriam?" the other asked.

"Um-hm," Paar answered.

"How about Randy? Did we wake Randy?" the first asked.

"Well," said Paar, coming out of the fog, "she doesn't sleep with us any more. There's just my wife, me, and Noel Coward here."

Another time, Paar attacked an exclusive New York tennis club for refusing to admit the son of United Nations immortal Ralph Bunche. Paar said, "If they let him in they're afraid they'll be overrun with Nobel Prize winners."

Paar began to get more and more political. In April of 1961 he talked at great length about the disastrous Bay of Pigs invasion the month before and forwarded the "Tractors for Freedom" idea. Paar wanted to trade tractors—which he felt Castro needed—for the prisoners Castro held. Paar felt that because he had been friendly with Castro and sympathetic to the revolution Castro would seize upon the offer. Then the prisoners would be released and the hard feelings between the United States and Cuba would be eased a bit and Jack Paar would have been the international diplomat who pulled it off.

For two weeks Paar and his audience waited for the welcoming words from Cuba.

Castro didn't even bother to reply.

In the fall of that year Paar got himself into another political set-to which could have become an international incident.

On August 13, 1961, the Communist East Berlin commander had closed the gates into East Berlin and had built a twenty-mile-long wall just inside the border to prevent the escape of East Berliners. Jack Paar, Peggy Cass, Miriam and Randy Paar, technicians and cameramen, decided to take a firsthand look at the wall and give viewers a firsthand report.

On September 12, 13 and 14, Paar reported on the Berlin crisis. He did a report from the Friedrichstrasse Gate, the one

American free-access road which was guarded but not sealed off to traffic. Jack and Peggy Cass stood fifteen feet from the dividing line and talked about the sadness of a city cut in two and the families that were divided. Jack was outspoken. The East Berlin soldiers took pictures of the Paar crew taking pictures. Jack interviewed two Army Colonels, an Army private who had been shot at with a Communist water cannon, refugees, and soldiers who were on duty at the wall. One of the Colonels demonstrated the Army's new rapid-firing M-14 rifle. Paar talked about a new radio personality in East Berlin who Paar said was an American defector. And finally they signed off with Jack saying, "We are not Pauline Frederick and Chet Huntley"—television newspeople of the time—"but more like Laurel and Hardy, but we tried to bring you the story of what is happening here."

Paar was accused of hoking up the act to create a private border crisis. The troops he had been interviewing, it was suggested, had been brought up to the wall specifically at Paar's request. So had machine guns and an anti-tank gun. It had made up one of the biggest displays of American armed might since the Berlin dispute started. Explaining away the sudden influx of troops at the wall, Paar said, "I am the best show in town," and when press indignation began to appear in the United States, Paar cracked, "It's going to get a hell of a rating for the show."

Most of the American press implied that Paar had used the U. S. Army for his own purposes and that he had endangered very delicate situations in Berlin. He had, according to one magazine, damn near turned the cold war into a hot one.

In the United States Senate, several members stood up and demanded that Paar be investigated and a special committee was suggested to do it.

Reporting on the furor, Paar said, ". . . before the [Berlin] show was shown on the air, the press carried certain stories implying my misuse of Army personnel and equipment. All hell broke loose about those reports, in the press, in the Senate, even in the White House—and all the uproar took place before anyone saw the show."

Emboldened by his adventures in international politics, Paar decided to go on to Russia just a week after the Berlin wall incident. Many viewers felt he shouldn't go behind the Iron Curtain; most particularly since Russia had recently exploded several nuclear bombs, which some interpreted as saber-rattling.

With Miriam and Randy and writer Paul Keyes and his wife, Paar took a commercial jet plane to Moscow. There they looked at new construction, shopped in the GUM department store, walked through the Kremlin, had lunch with the American ambassador, took pictures of sights which Russian officials allowed him to view (and had two rolls of exposed film stolen before leaving the city) and, in general, toured the city as tourists and not as newsmen.

When the Paars and the Keyeses had left Moscow and were safely back in the U.S. where no mouthing-off could provoke an international dispute, the American State Department let out its breath.

Paar came back to New York fighting mad. He was furious about the magazine and newspaper and broadcast reports of his Berlin confrontation tactics. He decided to take on the press, the Senate and even the White House, if necessary.

He began his counterattack on October 4, starting with his pet hate, columnist Jack Gould. He said that Gould had "led the literary lynching to a great extent, prejudging what he thought I did from inaccurate news reports. Mr. Gould threw many low blows at me and I have stepped aside, and they have curved, and if Mr. Gould will look he will discover before this show is over he has given himself a hernia."

Warming up to the job, Paar then took on "all the members of the Senate who raised their loud voices about this incident. All of them together do not have the decorations of this one fine Army officer." The officer was John Dean, one of the two Colonels who had been suspended from their posts for assisting Paar in Berlin.

Paar then reminded the press that he wasn't afraid of them.

"I have pointed to you that no one else . . . [what] no one else has ever done before, and that is, I have made Walter Winchell, Dorothy Kilgallen, Lee Mortimer and the rest of that ilk a laughingstock in this country. They have been defanged . . . and wisely they don't even mention me any more.

"Some members of the fourth estate act like members of the Fourth Reich."

Paar also challenged the United States Senate to investigate him all they wished but he said he would not be tried by them just as he would not be tried by the yellow journalists of the press. He attacked *Life*, *Newsweek* and the New York *Journal-American* for inaccuracies. He called the *Journal-American* "one of the most irresponsible papers perhaps in the country. It is also a warmongering newspaper . . . and when they don't have a warmongering going on then they have got some sexy trial that they are milking pretty good."

He also attacked the Chicago *Tribune* and its founder, Colonel McCormick, and later said he awarded that paper the "Poop-lutzer Prize—for yellow journalism." Then he turned on Chicago *Sun-Times* columnist Irv Kupcinet, as "one of the guys I replaced on this show before me which had no audience, no rating, no sponsors . . . run completely by news columnists."

Talking about Kupcinet, Paar said that a couple of years before Kup had been involved in something rather unpleasant and went into an aspect of Kup's personal life.

Hugh Downs unexpectedly attacked Paar.

"I don't think what you did in Berlin was wrong," Downs said defensively, "I think part of what you did tonight was wrong . . . when you slap at injustice or inaccuracy . . . in the newspapers . . . this is not only your right but I think your duty as an important person in this medium . . . but to attack on a basis that you did a guy like Kupcinet, who is a friend of mine, I think it is off base. . . . When you attack injustice, when you attack principles that are wrong you do so more effectively by not putting it on a personal basis. That's what grieves me . . . you don't need it."

To viewers, to guests, to members of the crew, it was becoming very obvious that Paar was becoming more strained, nervous and overly emotional.

Shortly after his tongue-lashing of the press, Paar announced that he was quitting the *Tonight Show*, not walking out to come back, but quitting for good. He revealed that NBC had offered him a new five-year contract, had offered to double his salary and had even offered him ownership of the program.

He blamed the tension and the exhaustion of doing the show as the main reason for abandoning it. He also said he was leaving because it was very difficult to find freedom of speech any more.

"If you don't believe me, let any union member . . . any little guy in a union—get up and say a few unpleasant truths about the big shots who run it. He'll see how far freedom of speech gets him; or try sometime at the next PTA meeting."

He said there should be more controversy in our land, more debates, more questions, more curiosity, more compassion and more honesty with ourselves and with others.

In an article which he wrote for *Look* magazine, Paar said:

"I . . . pride myself on the fact that no one has yet trapped me in any falsehood on my show. I've said things that are vengeful, even childishly vengeful. But I have never lied."

He gave NBC until March 30, 1962, to find a replacement for him. Commenting on their floundering around, he wrote, "They [NBC] have looked, held meetings, but as of now, they have not found anyone. So, if you know of anyone, please get in touch with NBC. There may be a finder's fee."

On March 29, 1962, comedian Jack E. Leonard opened the last original show of the Jack Paar *Tonight Show*. For fifteen minutes Leonard introduced celebrities who had dropped in to say good-by: Tom Poston, Sam Levenson, Selma Diamond, Jack Haskell and even Max Asnas of the Stage Delicatessen.

Following this, Jose Melis played a medley of theme songs from the Jack Paar show and Hugh Downs read comments about the show from Abel Green's column in *Variety*, the trade paper.

At eleven-thirty Paar came on stage to a standing ovation from the audience. He pointed out that they were coming to the end of 24,000 hours of programming and he showed some of the commercial products that had been sold successfully on the show. They cut to film clips of products that didn't work right during the commercials: a vacuum cleaner that wouldn't shut off, the Bufferin bottle, a motorcycle that was supposed to assemble in thirty-five seconds but wouldn't.

Then the producers showed a film clip taken in Cuba shortly after Castro took over. Paar then talked about his contacts with Cubans, his "Tractors for Freedom" campaign and his fights with the press.

Hugh Downs showed film and tape segments of people saying good-by to Jack Paar. George Burns, Jack Benny, Bob Hope, Joey Bishop, Shelley Berman, Nipsey Russell represented the comedians. Robert Kennedy and Richard M. Nixon represented the world of politics. Charles Laughton and Tallulah Bankhead represented the actors. Geneviève and Robert Morley represented the old talkers from the early Paar show, Billy Graham represented the church, and a technician represented the stage crew.

Opera singer Robert Merrill then closed out the show singing "Pagliacci" while Jack Paar said good-by, tears streaming down his face.

A slide came on and said, No More to Come.

The *Tonight Show*'s loudmouth, roughhouse years were over.

☆ **9**

"You remember our first failure on the *Tonight Show*," Mort Werner smiled. The program directors from the NBC stations turned to each other, grinned and applauded. Werner had put up a picture of Steve Allen.

"Everybody told us he was a failure when we hired him," NBC network's programming chief said, amused. "All of you who carried the Steve Allen *Tonight Show* know exactly what kind of failure he was."

For all of them, the Allen years had been moneymaking times. Werner had them hooked with his irony-clad approach.

"Then, of course, you all remember our next failure," he moved on.

He put up a picture of Jack Paar.

"When we hired him, the doomsayers told us he

wouldn't last six months," Werner said, "and that the *Tonight Show* wouldn't last long either."

He continued, "Well, you all know how badly Jack Paar and the *Tonight Show* failed." He smiled.

The television station executives applauded, thinking of the sold-out, golden hours they had during Paar's later years.

But now Paar was leaving the show and so were the viewers and the advertisers.

"Gentlemen, I'd like you to meet another failure. One who has been around a lot, who has flopped at a lot of things he's tried, and who, I am told, can't possibly succeed with the *Tonight Show*. Well, we think he can not only succeed but even top, yes, top, the amazing programming and profitability of the Steve Allen *Tonight Show* and the Jack Paar *Tonight Show*."

He uncovered a picture of a slat-thin young man with a leering smile. "His name is Johnny Carson, gentlemen, remember it. Tens of millions of Americans will never forget it."

"Who?" said one program director, turning to his boss.

"Johnny Carson, the kid over at ABC on that game show," he answered.

"What do I need that for?" Carson asked when he was first approached to take over the Jack Paar job on the *Tonight Show*.

Carson had just started his fifth—and last—year as host of the daily half-hour *Who Do You Trust?* show on the ABC network. The idea of adding an hour and fifteen minutes of live television a day to his work load wasn't Carson's idea of onward-and-upward. "Why me?" he asked.

Somebody told him he fitted Mort Werner's description perfectly.

Werner had said, "Allen, Paar and Carson have one thing in common: they have all done everything that can be done in broadcasting. They don't need prepared material or re-

Paar and Elsa Maxwell

Paar and Eleanor Roosevelt. Robert Morley seated left.

NYC Mayor John Lindsay and Johnny Carson

Jonathan Winters (substitute host) with
Dodie Goodman, Denise Darcel, Claude Stroud

Steve Allen, Pat Marshall and Steve Lawrence

Paar "Famous Baby" Act

Top left: Paar with Alexander King

Bottom left: Paar with Cliff Arquette and Geneviève

Below: Paar with Hugh Downs

Steve Lawrence, Jayne Meadows, Andy Williams, Steve Allen

hearsals. . . . The *Tonight Show* is the open forum of the
entertainment world, which makes it tough to control and it
also has a unique and complicated business construction.
The man who is running it has to know, first and foremost,
how to drive the train. He has to know when to stop for
commercials, where to go when he starts up again, and how
to keep the train on the track. . . . All we ask is that he de-
vote his whole life to the program."

NBC offered Carson a bit over a hundred thousand dollars
a year to do the show. They also offered to wait the six
months until September when his ABC contract ran out.

The thirty-seven-year-old comedian walked around the opportunity for two weeks, poking it with a toe every now and
then to see if it still pushed back. He compared it to the soap
opera-sandwiched daytime game shows he had been doing, to
the sit-in-for-somebody seats he had been warming, and to the
nice-young-man-next-door situation comedies he was being offered. Finally he decided to take it. His agreement came just
in time to head off any mass desertion of the premises by the
Tonight Show advertisers. NBC's main problem now was to
keep the franchise going six months until Carson signed in.

Between the March 30 good-bys of Paar and the October 1
hellos of Johnny Carson, an improbable assortment of ac-
tors, dancers, singers, announcers and comedians baby-sat the
Tonight Show. Taking a whole week's work or sometimes a
split one were Art Linkletter, Joey Bishop, Bob Cummings,
Merv Griffin, Jack Carter, Jan Murray, Peter Lind Hayes,
Soupy Sales, Mort Sahl, Steve Lawrence, Jerry Lewis, Jimmy
Dean, Arlene Francis, Jack E. Leonard, Hugh Downs,
Groucho Marx and Hal March.

Sponsors came and sponsors went. They came for the upcoming Carson show but went during the spring and summer
seasons. By the end of July the upcoming Carson *Tonight
Show* was completely sold out to twenty-nine sponsors. During the summer, however, more than half the advertisers
dropped out and NBC's late night revenues plunged.

Backing up the interim hosts that summer were Skitch Henderson and the orchestra and announcer Hugh Downs. Downs stayed until early August and then moved to the *Today Show*. He was replaced by Ed Herlihy.

"Vamping" is a show-business term that means waiting for a performer to catch up. NBC was doing a half-year vamp, waiting for Carson. Knowing the full-time job was already filled, the day-labor hosts made no great effort to make the interim *Tonight Show* a great effort.

Eva Gabor and Jack Carter once danced the twist. That was the highlight of the night.

An actor who said everything backward was the star of another night.

A really big attraction was Al Stevens and his talking dog.

One night disintegrated into ninety minutes of continuous, uninterrupted plugs for the participants. Henry Morgan plugged his new book and his summer stock appearances. Jonathan Winters plugged his new album and his new motion picture. Charlie Manna plugged his new album. Bennett Cerf plugged a new book and the *What's My Line?* show. Peter Lind Hayes, the host, plugged his summer appearances. And Leon Bibb, even managed to plug his new recording by label name and price.

A typical "exciting" show had an actress named Miiko Taka, comedy writer Carl Reiner, comics Bob Newhart and Dave Barry, singer Jack Jones and some film of the Holy Land taken by the show's host, Art Linkletter.

By late September, just before Carson's debut, the show had shrunk to a guest list of Hollywood producer Mervyn Le Roy, comedienne Pat Carroll and Nicolle Maxwell, a witch doctor—all still under the fixed chortle of genial Art Linkletter.

Meanwhile, the NBC promotion men were clacking it up for the young man with the shoe-button eyes, loving-cup ears and the fastest tongue in the east. The fourth coming of

Tonight got more press than the Second Coming of Christ might earn.

Finally, it was T-night! Millions of Americans stayed up to see NBC's new night watchman. Groucho Marx flew in from California to introduce him, although many viewers didn't know who Marx was. On hand to squeeze Carson's hand were Joan Crawford (who was terrified of appearing on a talk show but, once on, liked it so much she wanted a show of her own), Rudy Vallee, Tony Bennett, comedy writer Mel Brooks, an actor named Tom Pedi, the Phoenix Singers, and the announcer Ed McMahon and the producer Art Stark from Carson's ABC show.

At one point in the evening Carson said something like, "Jack Paar was the King of late night television. Why don't you all just look upon me as a Prince?" He was later to regret that line.

From the very beginning Johnny had something for everybody. The Chamber of Commerce types accepted him as the young innocent. But the "with-it" (read hip or hep) crowd just knew he was one of "theirs" when he got off a good one.

"Remember, Johnny, your body is the only home you'll ever have," Mr. America said to him one night.

"Yes, my home is pretty messy," Johnny shot back, "but I have a woman come in once a week to clean it out."

Show-business veterans, especially those who hadn't got the job, tuned in to watch Carson fail and were very surprised to find themselves laughing. They were also surprised at how well he handled himself and the show.

One night comedian Shelley Berman had been hogging the cameras and tediously talking about himself long after his time was up.

"You know, Johnny, I was an overnight star—" he said.

"Sure, Shelley," Johnny cut in, "but . . . not . . . tonight."

The first week he took over the *Tonight Show*, Carson

played to over seven and a half million viewers. He had 40.9 percent of the television viewing audience. Jack Paar had topped that only once—with a 48—the night he returned following his famous walkoff.

Carson ended the first month with an average of a little less than seven million viewers and twelve thousand pieces of mail, "most of it sex propositions or, as a second choice, a request for tickets to the show," said one of his assistants.

One of Carson's early plans was for first-person-adventure film sequences for the show. The week before the initial show, Carson dressed up in a baseball outfit, took the mound at Yankee Stadium and pitched against Mickey Mantle, Roger Maris and Elston Howard of the New York Yankees. That film was shown on October 5, as the first in a series of "dream sequences." A month later Carson went to Nellis Air Force Base in Nevada and flew with the Thunderbirds military aerobatic team to get some exciting footage.

On Christmas Day he showed a sequence of himself masquerading as Santa Claus in New York's Macy's department store.

"He was the regular George Plimpton of his day," one writer remarked.

By the end of the year Carson's *Tonight* was a must-do for the arrived and the still traveling. Tallulah Bankhead, Count Basie, Jack Benny, Carol Channing, Tony Martin, Adolphe Menjou, Agnes Moorehead, Mitch Miller, William Saroyan, Andy Williams and dozens of others had appeared.

Balancing off all these main attractions were the sideshow acts. Like the *Look* All-America football team, artist Salvador Dali, soft-drink salesman Commander Whitehead and a singer with a voice as big as her nose named Barbra Streisand.

When asked what he thought of Carson's opening month, Jack Paar said he went to bed early but what little he saw he liked. Paar went on to add that he, personally, had recommended Carson to the network.

Carson had a different approach to the subject of Paar. "Paar works emotionally. I work intellectually. Controversy is easy. I could make every front page in the country tomorrow by knocking Kennedy or coming out in favor of birth control."

The major difference between the two was described another way by an NBC executive: "Paar brought us an anxiety neurosis," he said. "Carson brings us a tranquillizer."

By February of 1963, NBC didn't need to be hit on the head to know they had a hit on their hands. The program had grossed more than seven and a half million dollars since Carson took over and it was sold out for a season ahead. Patting him on the back while ushering him into a chair, executives of the network signed him to another full year on the show.

"Oh, good," said the assistant director in charge of special demonstrations, "now we can do more skin diving, pogo stick jumping, bullwhip cracking, Siamese dancing and yoga meditation," all of which Carson had done during assorted shows.

Early in 1963, Carson did his imitation of Jack Paar and attacked a performer on the air. The professional pill-taker and pianist, Oscar Levant, had appeared on a February 8 Jack Paar "special." During the Paar show Levant commented on the current *Tonight Show* and offered the opinion that Johnny Carson was "amiably dull."

Three nights later Carson accused Levant of being "obviously sick," and said that Levant probably watched the *Tonight Show* on radio.

Later that month Carson and one of his guests, John Bubbles, walked off the show because another guest, comedian Jackie Mason, had "taken over the show."

For a month there it was like old Paar.

Producer David Merrick verbally attacked New York *Times* critic Howard Taubman one night. Another evening Tallulah Bankhead attacked Governor George Wallace of her home state, Alabama. And a few nights later World War I ace and airline president Eddie Rickenbacker accused the Kennedy Administration of being Socialists.

In early August, Johnny Carson took a little time off to marry a tiny, green-eyed model named Joanne. That was the first Johnny's viewers were to hear of her, but not the last.

Six months later the show was steadily drawing three and a half million homes a minute by showcasing people like Danny Thomas, Rod Serling, trial attorney Jake Ehrlich, Woody Allen, José Ferrer, Harry Belafonte, Liberace and Sammy Davis, Jr.—for whom they once taped a show unusually early so he could make his opening night curtain at the Broadway production of *Golden Boy*. People couldn't get enough *Tonight* so NBC decided to add a sixth weekly show: a rerun on Saturday nights.

Nineteen sixty-four was an election year. It was also a big year for politicians on talk shows.

Los Angeles Mayor Sam Yorty came on the program to complain about garbage disposal in Los Angeles even though he was in charge of it. Writer Gore Vidal appeared to talk about Governor Rockefeller, Robert Kennedy, Barry Goldwater, and even said that he thought "the Republicans would run Nixon so they wouldn't have to break in a new loser."

One night the announcer opened the show by saying, "And now heeeeere's John," and out came New York Mayor John Lindsay.

Carson also broke in a night club act at the Sahara Hotel in Las Vegas. He sang a song, told a few jokes, talked about his show and broke the house record—set by Judy Garland two years before.

More than fifteen hundred people a night drove up to four hundred miles and stood in line up to three hours and paid a hefty cover charge to see a man they could see six nights a week at home free.

Late in 1964, Carson introduced the *Look* magazine All-America team on the show. It may have been the most bumper crop of the decade. Nearly all of the young players went on to become professional football greats including Donny Anderson of Texas Tech, Fred Biletnikoff of Florida State, Jack Snow of Notre Dame, Steve DeLong of Tennessee, Tommy Nobis of Texas, Dick Butkus of Illinois, Tucker Frederickson of Auburn, Floyd Little of Syracuse, Craig Morton of California, Jerry Rhome of Tulsa, Gale Sayers of Kansas and a dozen others.

By early 1965 the strain had begun to work on Carson and he showed it. Struggling to put on seven and a half hours of programming a week, Carson once cracked that he needed a vacation and was negotiating with the International Red Cross to get him one. A particular point of distress to Carson was the extra fifteen-minute segment of the show done from 11:15 to 11:30 P.M. for those stations in the network line-up that had nothing to fill in there.

In protest, Carson arrived on two shows fifteen minutes late and let Ed McMahon talk his way through Carson's tardiness. Carson called his late arrival a "fifteen-minute virus" and said he wouldn't do the extra segment any longer. He pointed out that even the NBC-owned and -operated New York station used those fifteen minutes for news, then at eleven-thirty cut in the *Tonight Show*. It took a full two years after Carson's fight, but the *Tonight Show* finally lined up all of its stations to start at eleven-thirty (ten-thirty in the Midwest).

The show began to get as structured as a Japanese kabuki dance.

On an average evening Ivan Tors would come on and talk about bottle-feeding dolphins, Eddie Fisher would talk about Las Vegas, John Forsythe about the Dodgers, then Harry Golden would tell accent stories, the national bubble gum champs or a drum and bugle corps would blow, and a starlet would appear and say her new flick "opens in two weeks—what date is that, Johnny?—and I'm allergic to cheap jewelry and the airlines think I'm only twenty so I fly half fare and buy my clothes in the children's department and I wore this dress because you missed it last time."

For a change of pace, Carson once booked a contest between a six-hundred-pound pig and a three-hundred-and-fifty-pound pony to see which was the smarter. Everyone thought it would be a hoofs-down victory for Misty, the pony.

The personable Misty shook hands on demand, counted with her hoof and answered questions by tossing her head.

The pig, Oink, looked disdainfully at Misty's performance and then took center stage. Oink rolled out his own performer's carpet, walked on his knees and sang a medley of "Popeye the Sailor Man" and "The Blue Danube Waltz."

At the beginning of 1966, Carson's *Tonight Show* was running a full fourteen Nielsen points ahead of Paar's best *Tonight Show* ratings. Carson was now up to a reported four hundred thousand dollars a year—his pay for keeping eight and a half million Americans awake an average of twenty minutes after their normal bedtimes. Although he was now backed by a total crew of more than seventy people, including his brother Dick, who directed the show, Carson took more and more of the program under his own wing.

Carson's weariness or boredom began to emerge. At home and at the studio he was testy, defensive, withdrawn and uncomfortable with people. Once when questioned about his attitudes, he snapped, "I'm friendly, aren't I? I'm polite, aren't I? I'm honest! All right, my bugging point is low, I'm not gregarious. I'm a loner. I've always been that way."

Some of the waspishness came out on camera. One night he said that writer-guest Selma Diamond had been voted Playgirl of the Month by *Popular Mechanix* magazine. He said Skitch Henderson came out on top in a Xavier Cugat look-alike contest and he said, about a newspaper columnist who once attacked him, that she was a living example for birth control.

The show continued to build new stars. Bill Cosby came on an unknown and left the show a nationally recognized comedian. So did a grinning, pleasant young man who had been a writer for Jack Paar and for Carson. His name was Dick Cavett. A superb vocalist named Ruth Price came out of the smoky clubs and showed Carson's viewers what good jazz sound was. Don Rickles and Norm Crosby joined the Bob Hopes and Kate Smiths on the panel and received the same exposure.

Carson continued attracting politicians. Vice-President Hubert Humphrey made a fifteen-minute appearance and told stories about Lyndon Johnson and Harry Truman and talked about campus rioters and Christmas presents he was going to send.

A week later Barry Goldwater visited the show and discussed the Indians of Arizona, the situation in Vietnam, his new book and Hubert Humphrey. "Listening to Hubert," he said, "is like looking at *Playboy* magazine with your wife turning the pages."

Illinois Senator Everett McKinley Dirksen also made an appearance to talk about his superpatriotic record album called *Gallant Men*. And a couple of days later Carson welcomed William F. Buckley, Jr., editor of the *National Review* and candidate for mayor of New York the year before. Buckley talked about riots, about politicians, about his own television show, *Firing Line*, and got off two side-of-the-mouth comments which were widely picked up and quoted.

He said, "You know, President Johnson could have run on the Goldwater ticket of 1964—he's mobile."

And he also said, "We've got to do something [in Vietnam] that the New York *Times* doesn't approve of—either win or get out."

The friendly politicians, the fawning motion picture stars, the $40,000-a-week appearances in Las Vegas—this was all heady stuff for a small-town boy from Corning, Iowa.

Johnny Carson was born there on October 23, 1925. His father, Homer Carson, was an electric company lineman and his job called for frequent moves throughout the Midwest.

When Johnny was thirteen years old he became curious about a magazine advertisement that promised he could "amaze and mystify" his friends easily and without a great deal of work. He sent away for a magic kit and practiced long and hard to master the tricks in the instruction book. By the time he was halfway through high school he was performing —for money—at Rotary Clubs, church benefits, corn festivals and local fairs. He was determined to become a professional magician like Houdini or Blackstone. Even today old friends and family tease him by saying, "Take a card, any card."

He went to the University of Nebraska and started his radio career in Lincoln and then, later, in Omaha. In 1951 he moved to California and sold himself into a staff announcer's job at station KNXT. He also was given a half hour of empty Sunday afternoon time to fill and he created a whimsical, light-hearted show called *Carson's Cellar.* The budget for the entire show was twenty-five dollars so it included a lot of Carson and very few paid guests. The free ones who showed up to visit didn't need the money. They were Fred Allen, Groucho Marx, Jerry Lewis, Jack Benny and Red Skelton. Soon Skelton hired Carson as a writer.

One day in 1954, Skelton ran into a breakaway door that didn't break away during the rehearsal. He was injured and couldn't go on but suggested they get Carson to take his place. Carson had two hours to get ready for the show and to prepare material. He did and was such an instant success that CBS gave him a full hour of prime network time.

They called the offering the *Johnny Carson Show* but left little up to Carson. Experts, advisers, directors, producers, programming executives moved in and planned the program for him. Dancing girls, they said, and pratfalls, they said, and spinning spotlights, they said, and lots of noise and music, they said. The soft comedy and intimate appeal of Carson disappeared. The show ran its thirty-nine-week schedule in 1955 and was dumped. From there, Carson sat in for the ill, the infirm and the vacationing hosts on other shows for two years until he landed the steady work of emceeing *Who Do You Trust?* He kept that job until he took on the *Tonight Show* in 1962.

By Carson's fourth year on the *Tonight Show*, the late night television business had become big business. Over two hundred twenty-six million dollars a year was being spent by advertisers to sell the red-eyed crowd. At CBS and ABC, the money men began asking the programming men why they weren't cashing in on this blabbermouth bonanza, now selling for seventeen thousand dollars a minute. One of the networks began to look around for a talk show host and settled on Joey Bishop. The other liked the looks and sound of a syndicated showmaster and ex-singer named Merv Griffin.

With sponsors waiting in line, Carson could afford to start using commercials as a springboard for comedy. His new Carson Players troupe began to do satires and spoofs of commercials and Carson leered at advertising claims in his monologues and often used slogans as straight lines leading into comedy.

One of the writer lines never used but typical of the humor was a take-off on the Virginia Slims cigarette campaign. "You've come a long way, baby," Carson was supposed to say, "but you still haven't come across."

Another one not used was "Ford has a better idea. Buy a Chevy."

Carson even went out of his way to attack dishonest advertising. One night Ed McMahon had just encouraged the audience to dish out a bowl of ice cream and top it off with some delicious Smucker's butterscotch topping.

Stepping up to the announcer, Carson asked, "How long will that take to melt?"

Diplomatically, McMahon tried to avoid the question. Carson pressed on and urged McMahon to sample the ice cream. "You've been talking about how wonderful it was. It does look wonderful on television," Carson said.

McMahon finally admitted that the "ice cream" in the bowl

was really lard and that actual ice cream wasn't used because the hot lights in the studio would melt it too soon.

"There ought to be a certain amount of honesty, you
know," said Carson sternly.

"When they show that woman cleaning that floor and say,
'One swipe to it,' did you ever see that floor? It's the filthiest
thing you have ever seen and they go right through. . . . They
put graphite on the floor, powdered graphite. . . . I don't
think that's fair," Carson said. The audience cheered. The
advertising men booed. For a moment there it sounded like
a replay of the best of Jack Paar.

Usually Carson took no sides, played no on-air politics.
He reasoned that if he came out in favor of school busing he
could lose many Darien, Connecticut, viewers but if he came
out for non-integrated schools he would lose other viewers.
He allowed both sides the right to his microphones and to
their opinions and tried hard not to look pained or dis-
believing when the radicals, militants or crackpots began
sermonizing on Carson's time.

During 1967 he encouraged Dr. Robert Ettinger to come on
the show and talk about the work being done in cold storage
of the dead. Dr. Ettinger pointed out that they could freeze
people who had just died from diseases until the world came
up with a cure for those diseases. Then the body could be
thawed, cured, and the individual would live on.

Father Kavenaugh came on to tell why he had left the
Catholic Church. Mrs. Moshe Dayan talked about Israel's
problems with the Arabs. Anton LaVey appeared to defend
his First Church of Satan and the black mass. Bishop James
Pike of the Episcopal Church appeared to talk about the
dogmas of Christianity in which he no longer believed. At
one point he rejected the Trinity because he said he couldn't
understand what spiritual substance was and how three persons could share it. Dr. H. Curtis Wood showed up to present
an argument for his book *Sex Without Babies* and William F.

Buckley, Jr., showed up again to yell at Congress for handing their problems over to the President.

Carson listened through it all, took no sides. He also avoided the face-to-face confrontations other talk shows promoted. When Gore Vidal and William Buckley battled, they had their own uninterrupted nights on the show to present their cases.

In March of 1967, Carson was forced into political action. The American Federation of Television and Radio Artists decided to get more money for newsmen in New York, Chicago and Los Angeles, to place standby announcers on FM radio stations and to reject the network rule that staff announcers had to retire at age sixty-five. When the networks, headed by NBC, turned down the demands, AFTRA officials notified their membership to strike against the broadcasters.

The *Tonight Show—starring Johnny Carson* went immediately to videotaped repeats from late 1966. These played nightly while the strikers waited for AFTRA and the networks to come to some conclusion.

On April 4, a week after the strike had started, NBC received a registered letter from Carson which said he was quitting. It said he was rescinding his contract because the use of repeat (tape) broadcasts during the strike was a breach of contract.

"Not so!" yelled NBC in protest. "The contract says we can."

The press chased Carson down, found him in Fort Lauderdale, Florida, and pinned him to the beach about future plans.

"Let's just say I'm an unemployed prince," Carson snapped at them.

All over the country, newspapers picked up the "prince" reference and sneered at Johnny's royalty affectation.

"What they had forgotten," Carson said later, "was that I had used that phrase on my first show—the night I said Paar was the King and I was just the Prince. The entire reference was misunderstood."

Carson's contract at the time paid him about fifteen thousand dollars a week and gave him thirteen weeks' vacation a year. The Carson show was pulling over twenty-five million dollars a year into the network.

There were early rumors that Carson was using the strike to get a "better" deal from NBC. The unofficial figure tossed around was "one million dollars better."

Carson had a new set of advisers at his side. He had fired his longtime personal manager, Al Bruno. (In one case, an aide reported, Budweiser beer had offered Carson a distributorship to do commercials for them. Bruno said cash was better and turned down the offer. The brewery made the same deal with Frank Sinatra, however, and that distributorship turned into a multi-multimillion-dollar property.)

Waiting it out, Carson said, "I like TV. I like what I have been doing. I don't think anybody is happy with the strike. Everything is out of context. . . .

"The whole thing seems so ridiculous. There's a war in Vietnam and a truck drivers' strike, and things like crime and poverty to worry about. Why is it so important whether Johnny Carson goes back on the *Tonight Show?*"

His comment sounded like a rewrite on Illinois Governor Adlai Stevenson's remarks about Jack Paar's walkoff.

Meanwhile, planning for the day the strike would be settled, the ABC network people were putting together their newest late night show. The host, Joey Bishop, had come up with the idea of doing the show "live" to recapture the spontaneity of talk shows. He also had lined up an impressive list of guests which included California Governor Ronald Reagan and the old roughhouse infighter, Jack Paar.

NBC threatened to replace Carson with Bob Newhart and Newhart sat home practicing his "Lincoln's adman" and "lost submarine" stories.

An outfit called United Network began to sell to independent television stations a syndicated late night show that originated in Las Vegas and was hosted by Bill Dana. Dana knew a little about late night shows. He had been a writer and performer (under the name José Jiminez) during the Steve Allen *Tonight* period.

When the strike finally ended, NBC sent Carson a telegram saying it expected him to report to work.

Carson didn't show up.

In fact, Carson didn't even reply to the telegram.

The first night after the strike, NBC played another repeat. Then they scurried around for a fast replacement, found Newhart was negative, and put a folk singer named Jimmy Dean behind the empty desk.

Dean was tasteless and obvious. He cracked wise about Carson's absence from the show. One time, as a joke, he read a wire that said, "I'm happy to announce my return next week to my show, signed . . . Jack Paar." Nobody laughed.

"You'd think pride of ownership in his show, if nothing else, would bring Johnny back," one of the executives commented.

The suspense ended when Carson's attorneys, Arnold Grant and Louis Nizer, announced that he would be back on the *Tonight Show* on April 24.

Among other things Carson said on his way back was, "I hope to repay their generosity with the best that is in me." Carson was talking about viewers who had missed him but could just as easily have been talking about the generous rewards he had received from NBC for coming back.

The contract terms were a closely held secret. "One of the terms was that nobody is to know the terms," someone observed.

But one of the negotiators revealed that Carson hit NBC for vacation pay, for insurance policies, for additional payments every time a show was rerun, and for a different corporate setup to produce the show. Carson could now hire and fire production people, control the show more closely and get a pay raise of over a million dollars.

One published report said that Carson was to be paid four

million dollars over three years or more than thirty thousand dollars a week.

Was whatever the settlement was worth it?

Carson's first show back whipped the living nighttime out of everything *TV Guide* could list in the same hours. The *Tonight Show* (with the advantage of eighty more stations than ABC's *Joey Bishop Show*) pulled more than forty-one percent of the television audience. A Rock Hudson movie attracted twenty-two percent, Merv Griffin on the Westinghouse network got sixteen percent and Joey Bishop and Jack Paar in combination wound up a weak twelve percent.

The combination of Paar and Bishop had been an attempt to blunt Carson's return. It backfired. Paar was gay, exciting, funny and walked off with everything but the orchestra's music stands. He told old stories: "I didn't know Mickey Rooney was drunk on my show until I noticed all the fruit flies around his head." And he took over the Bishop show with new questions: "Ah, you know Sinatra's new wife," he attacked Bishop. "What's she like? She's very young, isn't she? Are they happy? Do you think it'll last?"

Joey Bishop blanched, gulped, followed meekly along behind while Carson controlled the time period and Bishop's guest, Paar, controlled the Bishop show.

Carson's popularity banged upward.

One night Carson left a suitcase full of turtleneck sweaters in the limousine NBC supplied to him. (The car-and-driver had been one of Johnny's earliest demands. "I'm not going to be caught on a rainy street late at night trying to get a cab while the audience comes out of the studio and attacks, screaming, 'Look! It's Him!'" he said to NBC.) The suitcase was stolen. Carson told the story on the air and said that the turtleneck he was wearing was the only one he had left.

Hundreds of turtlenecks began arriving. There were long-sleeved ones, short-sleeved ones and dickies. There were hand-knit, hand-crocheted and machine-made ones. There were wool, silk, nylon, rayon, cotton, satin, chintz and pongee ones. They came in eight shades of blue, six shades of pink, two reds, five grays, eight yellows, three whites, and one each chartreuse, burnt umber and Dayglo green.

Other mail brought dozens of portraits of Carson in needlepoint, in oils, in pastels, in macramé, in tiles, in sand castings, in collages, in oil-colored snapshots taken from the tube and in original paint-by-the-numbers cards.

Not all was fan mail. Two letters came in threatening his life and were turned over to the FBI. Six letters came containing strange symbols and blood-soaked pieces of toilet paper.

All was going very well. Shortly after Carson's return to the network he changed producers, fired Art Stark, the man who had been with him the many years on the ABC show. He replaced Stark with a man named Stan Irwin. Irwin's background was not television. He had been Executive Producer of the Sahara-Nevada Corporation in Las Vegas at one time and was the man who had arranged for Carson to make up to forty thousand dollars a week in his Las Vegas appearances.

Irwin and Carson decided to have a fifth-anniversary show —highlighting the bright points of the programs since 1962. Made up of film clips and kinescopes and tapes, the show was a collection of choice rehearsed and spontaneous bits through the years.

One sequence had Carson in a mock barroom brawl with Doug McClure and James Drury. Another showed him dressed as Shirley Temple and singing a satire called "On the Good Ship U.S.A." as a commentary on Shirley Temple's run for Congress. Films showed Carson quarterbacking a football team, sky diving and balloon soaring. He spoofed popular commercials. And finally they showed the famous tomahawk-throwing sequence. In that incident, actor-singer Ed Ames (who played the Indian, Mingo, on the *Daniel Boone* television show) said that he knew how to throw a tomahawk and would demonstrate. They set up a dummy. Ames said,

"Here's how you get rid of an enemy," and threw the tomahawk.

It landed neatly and firmly in the dummy's crotch.

The same spot where Carson and his *Tonight Show* now had NBC and the country's late night viewers.

☆ **10**

When a man in the studio audience complained that Carson kept his wife from coming to bed, Carson leered back, "Why don't you put on a better show than I do?"

It would be a tough assignment.

Smiling, pushing, chortling, prodding, listening, adding, probing and always topping the ever moving mouths of his guests, Johnny Carson had become the undisputed prince of America's darkness. By 1968, more than one out of three television sets lit up late at night were tuned to the *Tonight Show*.

As a reward for punching up NBC's midnight marauder, viewers might see a Broadway producer call a New York *Times* critic a washroom attendant or he might hear a guest say that another guest's miniskirt revealed "more than the poor girl actually has," or he might hear a city official accuse the CIA

of murdering President John F. Kennedy, or he might watch
the program try to keep our cities from becoming bloody
battlegrounds.

Nobody—not Johnny, not the producers, certainly not the
censors—knew what might be said on the *Tonight Show,*
especially by government officials, or by politicians or by the
people who live by and with and off of them. In an election
year, exposure is important and 1968 was an election year.

Although the *Tonight Show* wasn't the only game in town,
it was the one with the biggest kitty. That was where anyone
who had anything political to say headed first.

In January a comedian named Mort Sahl, who drained his
humor from the day's newspapers, said he was tired of hear-
ing new theories about the 1963 assassination of President
John F. Kennedy. Sahl was complaining about the district
attorney of New Orleans, Louisiana, a man named Jim Garrison. Garrison was saying openly that the Central Intelligence
Agency was involved in the killing of the President. Sensing a
good show, Carson invited Garrison to come on *Tonight* and
explain his theories.

A few weeks later Garrison showed up and sat at Carson's
side for almost an hour. He explained what they were doing
in New Orleans to clear up the "mystery" of the Kennedy
murder. Garrison said that the late President had been killed
by at least seven men. He pointed out that witnesses saw gun-
smoke coming from a grassy knoll along the line of parade. He
had a witness who had seen Jack Ruby driving a truck which
carried a gunman, and this witness had also identified Ruby
within twenty-four hours after the shooting—long before Ruby
killed Oswald in the Dallas City Jail.

Garrison went on to say the Warren Commission Report
was entirely untrue. The evidence was strong, he maintained,
that Kennedy was shot in the front of the head—the film
taken by a parade bystander named Zapruder showed the impact of the shots hurling the President backward. Garrison
rushed along, words, names, places, dates and times tumbling

over each other as he made point after point and ticked them off on his fingers.

Garrison said that there are four pages just listing files that must be kept secret, by order of the President. These files, according to Garrison, show a connection between Lee Harvey Oswald and the CIA and between the CIA and Jack Ruby. He said that a witness on the fourth floor of the Texas Book Depository didn't see anyone go up or down the steps after the shooting and that he had other witnesses who placed Oswald on the first and not the fourth floor of the building at the time the shots were fired.

He was most angry when he talked about the Parkland Hospital doctors' report and the autopsy sheets. "It was the first autopsy in history where the doctors' notes were burned!" he shouted.

He wound down by saying that, although he had only six men and the Warren Commission had six thousand men, he would bring out the truth that had been carefully covered up by the Commission, by the CIA, by the Dallas police and others involved in this ghastly conspiracy.

NBC and Johnny Carson learned two valuable facts that night. They learned that good, honest controversy—without confrontation—was good for ratings and for excitement. The Garrison appearance pulled hundreds of thousands of additional watchers to the *Tonight Show*. It was the one big subject people talked about at offices, in factories and at home the next day.

NBC and Carson also learned more about who was watching the *Tonight Show*. And why.

The network theory was that late night television was watched by undersexed middle-aged couples, teen-agers with one eye on a textbook, those who couldn't sleep, lonely people, night workers—like doormen—with undemanding jobs, solitary bar drinkers, and show folk who went to bed late and slept till noon. There was also, they guessed, a large

batch of people who had the TV on but who were off themselves, sound asleep in a living-room chair.

What new NBC studies showed was that the people who
turned on the *Tonight Show* were upper- and middle-income,
well-educated and interested in talking. The study pointed out
that factory workers had to be up early so they went to bed
early. Furthermore, those people with less education headed
for the monster movies late at night and not the witty, wordy
wisdom of the *Tonight Show*.

These days no reasearch is done without getting into the
motivations behind the statistics. The parapsychological motivations behind Carson's appeal, according to the parapsychological researchers, was that the host was homey and comfortable, so the audience was relaxed with him. However, he
also played the "who-me?" lecher. The unexpected leers and
sexual remarks tickled the viewers because they were on the
virginal white tube of television and also because they came
from an innocent-appearing face. For millions of men, he was
the cutup at the Junior Chamber convention. For their
women, he was the combination of son and lover. Most importantly, he was familiar and people at home called him
Johnny and felt they knew him as a friend or relative. They
seldom called Jack Paar or Milton Berle or even television's
all-time greatest talk show star, Arthur Godfrey, by their first
names, but to them Carson was Johnny—"Johnny said" or
"Johnny did last night."

Too, his relationship with announcer and old-time friend
Ed McMahon gave the home audience the idea that he was a
pleasant and warm person. Carson and McMahon had met in
1954 on the *Who Do You Trust?* ABC daytime game show
and when Carson moved to NBC and *Tonight* in 1962, he
asked McMahon to come along. On camera, McMahon
played straight man to Carson, smiled a lot, handled some
commercials and offered a comment here or there. When the
cameras shut down, McMahon did the leading. There was a
time when Carson was drinking "pretty good" as they say at

NBC's Hurley's bar (something he no longer does) and McMahon often went along, belt for belt. Each has blamed the other for getting his consumption up. Today, Carson drinks very little. He stopped because the need for liquid support seemed to vanish as his show became more and more successful. He also quit because his body couldn't take it any more and a few drinks could make him instantly intoxicated or bring on sudden physical reactions: chills, sweating, nausea. One doctor at the U.C.L.A. Medical Center in California says this could be a definite disease, one the medical group lightly calls "martini poisoning."

Tonight has done well by McMahon. He is president of del Sol Productions, a design company which produces sunglasses, greeting cards, industrial films and television commercials, most of them starring Ed McMahon. He also plays in summer stock, has done several 45-rpm recordings, appeared in a movie, and even gets an extra income for holding down his weekend warrior Colonel job in the Marine Corps Reserve.

The night Garrison appeared, Jack Haskell was substituting for McMahon. McMahon once said it was one show he was sorry to have missed.

Carson was sorry he was out of the seat during two history-making shows early in 1968.

Harry Belafonte was substituting for Carson on February 5 when New York State's Senator Robert F. Kennedy sat down to visit for a half hour. He started out lightly by saying that the current movie hit, *The Good, the Bad and the Ugly,* "refers to President Johnson, Gene McCarthy and myself." Then he began to talk about the Economic Opportunity Program, the frustrations in Watts, and the Black Nationalists' attitudes. He told a story about a young black boy who went to city hall to complain about the lack of garbage pickup. The boy was told that he had to be twenty-one years old to enter a complaint.

Kennedy said that our young people were disillusioned,

that innocents were being killed by the war, and that although he had an animosity toward President Johnson the war was a delinquent child. He ended with a josh, by talking about his recent journey to the Amazon River. "Forty-seven percent of the people were hoping I would fall in that river," he finished.

Three nights later Dr. Martin Luther King came on the program for close to a half hour. He talked about the serious problems facing this nation's poor communities, where unemployment was at a depression level. He talked of the guns-and-butter philosophy and said he planned a Poor People's March on Washington that spring.

"It takes half a million dollars to kill each Viet Cong," he said, "but we have only fifty-three dollars a year to spend on the poverty-stricken."

The war, according to King, was unjust and ill considered. The sit-in host, Harry Belafonte interrupted him to say that all his guests that week were against the war and for the civil rights movement. (Guests that week included Sidney Poitier, Petula Clark, Dionne Warwicke, Paul Newman, Buffy Sainte-Marie and Thomas Hoving, director of the New York Metropolitan Museum of Art.)

King closed by saying that he was now thirty-nine years old and that he had been twenty-seven when he first began this movement with a bus strike in the South. Then he was asked if he was ever afraid for his life.

"It isn't important how long you live. It's important how well you live," he said.

Martin Luther King hadn't much longer to live.

About six weeks after his appearance (when Johnny was off again and Sammy Davis, Jr., was sitting in for him) Ron Karenga was invited to appear on the show. Karenga, a hostile black militant, showed up with a guard of large, dashiki-dressed militants on either side of him. When he met with the production crew to talk about that night's show he threatened to lay out "the honkies" and to show the country that the black man was ready to fight for his rights. There were hurried discussions in the halls, frantic telephone calls throughout the RCA Building and mention of canceling Karenga.

"Controversy is all well and good," said the NBC censor, "but a whole show of bleep I don't need."

Karenga and his troops arrived for the dinner-hour taping of the show, keeping their dark sunglasses on even in the studio gloom. They sat silently, staring malevolently at the crew, at a comedian named Carl Barry who was on the show and at the other guest, dancer Ray Bolger. They nodded to popular singer "brother" James Brown. The ominous silence around them spread and the crew tiptoed around quietly instead of running, and the horseplay died out. Everyone on stage was wary, watchful, some even felt an involuntary shudder down their backs.

But the halls of NBC were not Ron Karenga's battle grounds. The looming cameras with the glowing red eyes, the snake patch of thick, greasy cables, the blinding lights, the quick-snapped directions into the headsets, the cut-flick-change of what was happening was too much. Obviously recognizing that his hostile attitude might not even sound serious but perhaps ridiculous in that atmosphere, Karenga went on the air with a toned-down approach. Although he presented some militant attitudes in words, he came off as controlled and sensible. At one point he even admitted that no group could do it alone and that we all, blacks and whites, militants and moderates, had to sit down together and agree to make this country work.

Upstairs, the NBC man in charge of the bleep machine took his finger off the trigger.

He needed it another night, however, when Carson took on the entire studio audience. That particular evening, Carson came swinging out, shrugged his shoulders to show the new outfit he was wearing, bowed to McMahon and the orchestra leader and headed off into his standard opening monologue. Halfway through the fourth punch line, he noticed the audience was sitting there, politely listening and not laughing. In fact, somewhere around the middle of the right side, he could even hear some hissing and a soft boo.

Not sure whether it was the microphone that was off or if it was his material, Carson decided to start over again. He walked off the stage, came back on again and yelled very loudly, "Go to hell," to the audience.

That didn't get a big laugh either, especially from the NBC censor.

On April 5, right after Martin Luther King had been murdered on a Memphis motel balcony, *Tonight* did part of the show about him. Sammy Davis, Jr., asked Carson if he could come on the show and talk to his black brothers. Carson opened up the time for him. The cameras moved in very tight on Davis when he asked the young Negroes around the country for calm and restraint in this, their hour of tragedy. He pointed out that there was nothing to be gained from violence.

"We are in a period of upheaval for black and white that is crucial to the country. We need to extend ourselves—and I hope the black brothers will take the next seventy-two hours to reflect on what Dr. King stood for. . . ."

He finished by asking the blacks to "cool it" and the whites to come forward and join the black brothers in friendship for the good of the country and the world.

Tapes of Martin Luther King's appearance the past February were shown. Millions watched as King, on tape, again talked about the poor blacks, about his Poor People's March on Washington, and the war in Vietnam. There was a chill when he answered, for all time, the question about being afraid for his life. "It isn't important how long you live. It's important how well you live."

The tapes were followed by Diana Ross and the Supremes singing "There's a Place for Us Somewhere."

Not every night was tragic. Sometimes the producers tried

to liven up the show by booking Pat Paulsen, a comedian who had decided to run for the Presidency, or one of the Gabor girls or even Jacqueline Kennedy's cook with gossip about green-salads-I-have-known.

Stan Irwin, the Las Vegas act booker who now produced the show, wanted to use a palsy-afflicted singer one night.

"You can't," one of the crew protested. "Look at how he shakes. That'll look terrible, just terrible."

Not to be denied, Irwin thought it over for a second, then said, "I know. Let's dress him in a sailor suit, give him a railing to hold onto and move the cameras like a rocking boat. That way nobody'll notice."

A few months later Irwin went back to booking acts and road shows—including Carson's out-of-studio personal appearances—and his job was inherited by an associate producer named Rudy Tellez. Some say Rudy got the job because of his ability. Others say Jeannie helped.

Jeannie Pryor, a tall, blonde lovely, had been Johnny Carson's private secretary for years. Her job included handling Carson's personal mail and telephone calls and callers. She also picked out his clothes for most shows and even appointed herself the hair stylist in charge of keeping Carson's hair brushed. She was always on him, brush in hand, after he had tried on wigs or wrestled with a judo champ or ridden a mechanical polo pony on the show.

One day Carson had asked her to model a mink coat on the program and, when she walked off, Carson turned to McMahon and said, "Did you know Jeannie's up to five words a minute in shorthand? And next month she's going to take a typing course." To the audience, Jeannie became an instant part of the family like McMahon and Doc Severinsen, the orchestra leader.

Two of the crew were trying to make Jeannie part of their families. The head talent coordinator—John Gilroy—and associate producer Rudy Tellez were both dating Jeannie. When

Irwin left the show, both young men were up for his job. Tellez got it. He also got Jeannie.

Encouraged by Jim Garrison's appearance, the talent co-ordinators searched around to find controversial guests. One night they invited Madalyn Murray O'Hair to talk, and talk she did, for a half hour. She had been waiting for a big, national platform and, once on it, began shaking her finger in America's face.

Madalyn Murray, as she was better known, was a well-publicized atheist. It was *her* Supreme Court case that ended with the student prayer ban in public schools. Her current hot topic was a fight to have church property taxed like any real estate. Her major anger, she said, was against the Catholic Church because it owned the most property. In naming the Catholic Church, she said most people didn't know it held stock in Dow Chemical (maker of explosives for the military) and that it had stock in radio and television and influenced our communications. She said the church did very little for the aged, the blind, the ill, that the job was done by the state and the cities, so why should the church be tax free?

The studio audience began shifting in their seats, one man booed, another hissed loudly and yelled, "Go back where you came from!"

Carson turned to her, a surprised look on his face, and said, "Are you used to these reactions?"

"First time it's happened," she answered. Carson frowned at the audience.

Within weeks, Carson had to frown again, this time at his guest. The guest was *In Cold Blood* author Truman Capote, who came on to "have a conjecture orgy" as one newspaper reported. Capote's subject was the killings of John Kennedy, Martin Luther King and Robert Kennedy. Capote was seized with the idea that it was all a master plot to disrupt the United States by slaughtering certain national leaders. The most disturbing part of his appearance wasn't the theory but

Capote's "rush to judgment" on who was guilty long before the courts had a chance to try the question.

He said, outright, that he didn't believe that James Earl Ray had killed Martin Luther King but that it was certain that Sirhan Sirhan had murdered Robert Kennedy. He also added that he thought it better for one innocent person to be punished rather than have a hundred guilty ones go free. If prosecution of the guilty can only be done at the expense of a certain percentage of the innocent, then let it happen, he insisted.

Normally undisturbed by the most outrageous remarks, Johnny Carson frowned, shook his head as though he hadn't heard right. He had. And so had the nation. The next day, newspapers attacked Capote's stand. They said that cases still being tried in the courts should not be second-guessed on television. They said that Capote had taken the law into his own hands and had, unjustly or illegally, influenced jurors. And one newspaper suggested that if Carson was going to let celebrities make random guesses on the guilt and innocence of trial defendants, then perhaps something should be done about freedom of expression on talk shows.

Carson's slight eye tic started to act up. It flicked when the newspapers rapped Capote's appearance. It was to become worse in future months.

It ticked its way through another visit from Hubert Humphrey ("Would you [Carson] like the job as Vice-President of the country?" Carson: "Yes"); New York Mayor Lindsay ("There is a relationship between the war in Asia and the riots in our cities"); Harold Glassen, president of the National Rifle Association ("Guns shouldn't be owned by the mentally ill, delinquents and criminals"); and Senator George McGovern ("I'm a candidate because . . . after the tragic death of Robert Kennedy, I thought his brother, Ted, would enter the race. . . . When he didn't I did, to take the positions of RFK").

It evidently didn't act up, however, when his brother Dick

came into his office one afternoon to quit. Dick had directed the show from the very beginning, and he now decided he wanted to go back to California to direct the new *Don Rickles Show*.

"Um-hm," said his brother, looking down at the jokes in his monologue for that night. "Listen, do you think we can get Bob Quinn to do it?" Quinn had once been Associate Director and Johnny Carson had always liked his way of handling the cameras and the show.

"And with that much of a goodbye from his brother, Dick Carson left," one writer observed.

There wasn't a lot of sentimentality around.

One Christmas, NBC asked Johnny's personal public relations man, Al Husted, what to get Johnny as a Christmas gift. Thinking about Carson's importance to the network and NBC's income of over two million dollars a month from the show, Husted suggested a custom clock.

"A clock?"

"Not an ordinary clock," said Husted, inspired, "but a great-looking clock from Tiffany's. And where the numerals are eleven and twelve o'clock, why don't we replace them with a special inset eleven-thirty in diamonds or something?"

"Hey, that's nice," said one of the network executives. "What's something like that cost?"

Husted shot back, all prepared, "It's twenty-three hundred dollars."

The executive thought it over for a moment, then countered, "How about a nice sweater instead? We had more like a hundred dollars in mind."

That cavalier attitude toward their biggest moneymaker could have been one of the reasons Carson reorganized his business matters during 1969. Reviewing what he had earned with what he had left, some said Carson began realizing that many of his "friends" were making off with his coat and wallet while he was off fighting to keep America tuned in to the *Tonight Show*.

One day Carson asked Sonny Werblin to meet with him. Werblin had been one of the financial powers at the giant MCA talent agency which was now out of business. The anti-monopoly people had lopped it apart because it controlled too much of the talent, the musicians, the writers, the producers and the facilities in television and motion pictures. Werblin had also made a lot of money as one of the owners of the New York Jets and still had blocks of stock or money in real estate, horses and financial institutions.

Listening to Carson's troubles, Werblin said he could help but Carson would have to cut him in. With no lawyers and no agents and managers to get in the way, Werblin and Carson signed papers making them partners forever.

Werblin immediately started to straighten out Carson's finances. He set up a full-time television production company called Raritan Enterprises, Inc., and told NBC it was taking over the complete production of the *Tonight Show*. It would be a "package" which NBC would buy from the two partners. Werblin also told the network that they wanted special arrangements made for Johnny to do specials and they wanted "development deals" in which Raritan would work on concepts for the network while the network underwrote them. Some of these extra-income projects for Carson turned out to be the TV specials, *Johnny Carson's Repertory Company in an Evening of Comedy* and *Johnny Carson Presents Sun City Scandals*.

They also asked for a block of RCA stock.

And Werblin even got Carson involved in the franchise craze with a line of fast-food restaurants which featured "Here's Johnny's Cole Slaw."

It was all a lot different for Carson than posing for a vodka advertisement, which he had once done for fast cash.

Werblin and Carson sat down with NBC to talk money and when they stood up NBC had a new contract that was good until 1973 and Carson was, according to a New York

Times report, "netting $75,000 a week," some of it in insurance and deferred payments.

Carson's eyelid started in again. He said the *Times* had run a "gross and ludicrous" exaggeration of his new contract with NBC. "It's damn unfair to me and damn unfair to performers," Carson complained. "I want to disclaim it once and for all."

The network said the *Times* was wrong, too.

Way off.

The right figure, according to people who know, is not that laughable seventy-five thousand dollars a week.

It is a much more reasonable and sensible fifty-five thousand dollars a week.

Plus insurance, stock, vacation pay and a piece of the profits from the hundred and fifty thousand a week which NBC pays Raritan for the program.

The home of the *Tonight Show*—studio 6-B in the RCA Building—was also redone for Carson. NBC spent two million dollars converting the original radio studio into a slick, electronics-crammed home for the *Tonight Show*. When it was finished, 6-B had four highly sophisticated RCA color cameras, a control room with twenty-three television monitors showing what the cameras were seeing, what the network was sending and what could possibly be added. It had enough lighting for the living rooms of four hundred homes. It had thirty-six loudspeakers located between the stage and audience and it had seventy different places on stage where a microphone could be plugged in.

With politics a dead issue by the beginning of 1969, the talent seekers began to search around for other controversial guests. They decided the biggest untapped pool of interesting subjects was in the 24,000 new books which are published every year. Irving Stone had always been popular. Sifting through the titles, the producers found new treasures to promote on the program.

Along with a car salesman named Ralph Williams and a

laser beam demonstration, the talent coordinators also invited Norman Mailer to come and bray about his muscular sexy books and Jacqueline Susann to simper about her frilly sexy ones. They had Johnny visit with Adam Smith and his book, *The Money Game*, with Arthur Hailey and his *Airport*, with Theodore White and his *Making of a President*, with Dr. Lawrence Peter and his *The Peter Principle*, and with writers like Jimmy Breslin, Judith Crist, Gloria Steinem, Buck Henry, Ellen Peck, Jerome Weidman, Lillian Hellman and Desmond Morris.

One night, as a change of pace, they booked another author. His claim to a seat on the show was that, in contrast to these best-selling authors, his book had sold only five copies.

The undisputed highlight of 1969 was a December wedding right on the stage of studio 6-B. Craig Tennis, a talented young writer-producer who was working as a coordinator, one day interviewed a hook-nosed, long-haired young man who hugged a shopping bag to his chest. His name was Tiny Tim, the popeyed oddity admitted, and he played the ukulele and sang songs "like they did in the twenties."

"The twenties?"

"Like Rudy Vallee and Nick Lucas."

"Nick Lucas?" asked Tennis.

"Well, you know," said Tiny Tim, warming up, "he sang 'Tiptoe Through the Tulips' in the film *Gold Diggers of Broadway* in 1929 and he sang 'Liza' while Ruby Keeler tap-danced in another 1929 film called *Show Girl*. That's what I do. I sing those songs like they were sung then."

Taking a deep breath, Tennis recommended the show have Tiny Tim on to strum his ukulele and sing "like Nick Lucas."

From the first falsetto note until his last soft good-by, Tiny Tim had millions of home viewers transfixed. Eyes popped open, jaws dropped, and people sat stock-still, forgetting refrigerators and toilets, while he smiled, minced, dimpled, strummed and sang.

"Jezus H. I never saw nothing like that," the country exploded after he went off.

"Did you see that freak?" insurance salesmen asked each other over coffee the next morning.

"He's cute," their secretaries sitting at the next table said.

"Is he for real?" asked advertising men, wondering if they could use him in a hairdressing or nasal congestion commercial.

"All the time," answered people who had seen him perform in dark, downtown cellar clubs.

"I think he's funny," said the Bucks County and Westchester and Evanston and Bond Hill and Westwood and Cedar Grove housewives.

"Then we'll have him on again," said the *Tonight Show.*

"You old star maker you." Tennis whistled a sigh of relief.

At one point, Tiny Tim announced that he was going to get married. Within earshot was the young publicity man, Al Husted. He suggested that Carson bring the subject up to Tiny Tim one night and then ask if he would like to be married right there, yes, on stage, with cameras whirring and all, on the *Tonight Show.*

Tiny Tim's hands fluttered to his chest. "Oh, could we?" His face beamed.

The wedding was set for a week before Christmas and NBC, sensing good video attendance at their social event of the year, set out to do things right. Tiny Tim had said that both he and his beloved, Miss (and he always called her Miss) Victoria May Budinger, "just loved" tulips.

"Get us some tulips," NBC ordered.

Tulips are not a winter flower. Faced with that unalterable natural fact, the *Tonight Show* producers thought about it for a moment and then sent out for some—all the way to Holland where tulip plants are stored at low temperatures to prevent blooming before they are mature.

They ordered ten thousand plants to be brought out of

their freeze three weeks before the show and then shipped to the NBC studio. Other crew people ordered in roses, carnations, Indian paintbrushes, lilies, laurel, wild grapes, peonies, poppies, mistletoe, lilacs, clover, black-eyed Susans, violets, hibiscus "and anything else the kids selling at a buck a bunch on the street have left over," someone cracked.

The press department at NBC sent out a mimeographed invitation to the wedding on the *Tonight Show* to the press but unfortunately the press didn't read it too carefully. Suddenly the press department, the producers of the show and Johnny Carson realized they had thousands of important requests for seats and only hundreds of seats available. *Time, Life, Newsweek* wanted to come. *Variety* and *Reporter* wanted to be there. So did *Women's Wear Daily, Tailor and Cutter, American Florist, Audio Engineer,* another TV network and even the Los Angeles *Free Press,* which claimed Tiny Tim as one of "theirs," whatever that meant.

Gene Walsh, the affable, able head of NBC's press department, and his pretty red-haired assistant, Trudy, were handed the job of separating the chaffed from the wheat. They turned away as many journalistic VIPs as they seated and even had NBC network vice-presidents standing in the outside corridor.

The wedding had more press coverage than all of Tommy Manville's, Lana Turner's, Ava Gardner's, and Frank Sinatra's combined.

One of the reasons for the high interest was the freakishness of the wedding. Not only was the fluttery, silver-voiced tenor getting married to a girl (which looked highly unlikely) but everything was done for maximum attention. For clothing, Miss Vicky settled on a "simple" $2500 Victorian wedding gown and the traditional borrowed old cameo, new Bible, and a blue garter.

The male of the species, however, would settle for nothing less than a black silk velvet frock coat, ribbed satin vest, satin shirt, striped pants, a flared-crown top hat and a black silk cape, all supported by a hand-carved walking stick.

While the minister was saying, "I now pronounce you man and wife," a rating service taking a fast "overnight" reading on the number of people watching pronounced NBC and the *Tonight Show* the absolute, undisputed owner of late night television and the people who watched it. More than one out of every two sets turned on was tuned in to the wedding.

Even over at CBS, Merv Griffin's crew watched the wedding on backstage monitors.

By 1970 the Prince had become the King. A nod of Carson's head could create a national hero. A frown could mean sudden death for an act. An invitation to appear and talk could mean overnight success and instant fame for comedians, for singers, for talkers and especially for writers. Publishers elbowed each other out of the way to get a book and an author on the show. Sometimes writers were picked because they were pretty or witty or had something exciting to say even if their books weren't too good.

In a short time the *Tonight Show* launched four books that sold millions of copies and frightened, excited, reduced and saddened the country.

A professor of biology at Stanford University appeared one night to talk about the population explosion. He said if the current trend continued there would be horrible disease and famine, that by 1975 we would have four billion people— that we are adding seventy million people a year to our planet, that in all the wars the United States had fought there had been six hundred thousand battle deaths—and that six hundred thousand people had been born in the last three days—that we are looting the earth of its resources—ten to twenty million people would starve to death—that we could lose a billion people to diseases—and now, he said, WE MUST STOP HAVING CHILDREN, BEFORE THE GOVERNMENTS ARE FORCED TO DESTROY THEM.

We must act to save the three and a half billion people we have now so we can save the three and a half billion to come.

Ehrlich's book, *The Population Bomb*, sold out overnight. Zero Population Growth proponents had the first major tide of interest in their movement. Schools, universities, hospitals, teachers and politicians talked about his appearance and quoted him. A sense of emergency fell across the country and the man in the street began to understand finally what the man in the mankind studies was talking about.

"The amazing thing about him," said one show member, "is he was talking people out of having kids—while they were lying in bed."

David Reuben, a doctor from San Diego, came on with his *Everything You Always Wanted to Know About Sex*, etc., book which contained information anyone could have found in *Popular Hygiene* and the Visiting Nurse Association pamphlet rack.

If it wasn't sex, it was how-to-be-beautiful, and another doctor, Irwin Stillman, visted the show to talk about his book, *The Doctor's Quick Weight Loss Diet*. It was an off-the-shelf best seller and Stillman started a diet-book factory by rewriting the successful formula into *The Doctor's Quick Inches Off Diet*, *The Doctor's Quick Teenage Diet* and others.

Today, Stillman is one of the world's best-selling authors. His book sales are in the millions. He doesn't need the *Tonight Show* any longer but he still appears every two months or so because, as one talent coordinator put it, "He's a charmer and can talk on many subjects. We like it if the author plugs his book once but if we have him back, we'd like him to talk about other subjects."

One author who could talk on many subjects was a Harvard faculty member named Erich Segal who had written a novel called *Love Story*. Segal mugged, hammed, simpered, grinned and quoted, alternately, *Love Story* and the classics to the show audience and sold more than a half million hardcover copies of his book. Other faculty members at Harvard sniffed, said that Segal had certainly gone Hollywood, which was not exactly true. Segal had always been that way, had even written the script for a Beatles film called *The Yellow Submarine.*

Other books got off to flourishing starts when their authors came on the show. Robert Townsend, who was never asked back because he accused NBC of being a monument to the Sarnoff family nepotism, sold many copies of *Up the Organization* through his one awkward exposure.

Merle Lynn Brown told people *where* to have sex in her book *The Ravishers.*

Henry Sutton sold *The Vector,* Jane Howard pushed *Please Touch,* Morton Hunt had luck with *The Affair* and Alvin Toffler became a nationally known and quoted expert with his appearance and his book, *Future Shock.*

But not only the writers used the Carson highway to peddle their own pushcarts. Jimmy Webb sold his songs, Graham Kerr pushed his *Galloping Gourmet* television show, Peter White sold tickets to *The Boys in the Band,* Joan Ganz Cooney explained the educational advantages of her *Sesame Street* television show and the Harlem Globetrotters tossed a ball around and announced their on-the-road appearance dates. Even the United States Government, through NASA, put an endless string of astronauts on the show to talk about places they had been or places they were going—to keep the public interest high in the space program.

Four or five a night, a score a week, hundreds a year— they pass Carson's way, sit to chat for anywhere from five minutes to an hour, and then move on again. The critics, the standups, the impersonators, the rock singers, the editors, the astrologers, the athletes, the hula hoop champs and the Ding-A-Ling Sisters.

"The best guests," Carson says, "are the uninhibited people . . . they know who they are and don't try to prove they're something else.

"The trick on this show is to try to avoid being dull, which is the worst sin of all. . . .

"When writers say that talk shows are all alike, they're wrong. They can't be all alike because you've got a different guy there, and what David Frost or Merv Griffin or Cavett do with a person, I might do completely differently."

What Carson has done is let them yak. Blab. Chat. Chin. Gab. Jaw. Drool. Gush. Yap. Shoot the bull, beat their gums, and chew the rag. He's had politicians proclaim, movie stars swear, doctors prescribe, sociologists warn, and leaders promise. He's showcased John F. Kennedy, Robert Kennedy, Martin Luther King, Sam Sheppard, John Glenn, Paul Ehrlich, Germaine Greer, George McGovern, Hubert Humphrey, Harold Glassen, Ron Karenga, Edmund Muskie, Jim Garrison, Madalyn Murray, Norman Mailer, Gore Vidal, Harold Hughes, John Lindsay . . . and over ten thousand others, all talking their guts out about something they want, something they need, something they believe is important for people to hear.

And, once a year, reviewing all of this on his anniversary show, Carson selects the highlights of the *Tonight* years.

It shows Carson sky diving, brawling in a barroom, spoofing commercials, singing a Shirley Temple song and Ed Ames throwing a tomahawk into a dummy's crotch and America's heart.

☆ **||**

Shirley Wood, Sy Kasoff, Shelly Schultz, Bruce Cooper, Rudy Tellez, Mike Zanella, John Gilroy, Silvia Pancotti, Craig Tennis, Perry Cross, Art Stark, John Carsey, Stan Irwin, Fred de Cordova, four or five others.

Except as a gag you won't see these people on the *Tonight Show*—but this is part of the group that decided whom you did see.

These are the interviewers, the talent coordinators, the directors and the producers who hand-picked the ever babbling stream.

Since the fall of 1962 they and others have singled out over ten thousand ingenues, fops, starlets, editors, bums, animals, authors, cops, fags, psychiatrists, pitchmen, actors, shills, singers, directors, horn blowers, dietitians, warriors, inventors, bellhops, sailors, gamblers, Australians, right tackles, hunters, faith healers, cab drivers, playwrights, cooks, gandy dancers, high divers, hoods, deans, flacks, hip shooters, mayors, practitioners, jockeys, and people who make cars out of junk, people who make junk out of cars, and a lot of other people who just let talk dribble out of their mouths, non-stop.

Their job is to find three, four or five devilishly fascinating or highly amusing or deeply intriguing guests each show—five shows a week, two hundred and sixty different shows a year.

Sometimes they hit it lucky. They find a Joan Rivers. Or a Flip Wilson. Erich Segal. Tiny Tim. David Reuben. Don Rickles. And listening to the balls of laughter rolling down the bowling alley RCA Building halls, they asked them back again and again and again. And then again and again and again.

They even had Shelley Winters back a lot although nobody knew what "Old Shel" was going to do or maybe that's why she always came back. Shelley drinks and fights and sometimes does both at the same time on the show. She yells, she weeps, she mopes, she shows her muscles some nights and other nights won't take off her mink coat and nobody insists she do so because they don't know what, if anything, she has on underneath it. One night she showed up on another talk show wearing shoes, a mink coat and a smile. Back to camera, she opened the coat so the host would understand that Shelley was a lot more than just talk.

Balancing off Shelley Winters is someone like Joan Rivers, who appears on time, stays sober, does her solo routines, gives Carson straight lines he can top and subjects he can mold. She meet the guests well, talks with them easily, has something to add on a thousand subjects and tries to help the show along and not drag her heels to slow it down.

There are guests they want but can't get like Greta Garbo or Howard Hughes or Pablo Picasso.

There are guests they can get but don't want like Ralph Ginzburg and Jane Fonda and Robert Townsend.

And every once in a while Shirley or Sy or Shelly or Bruce or Rudy or Mike or John or Silvia or Craig would find a dream of a guest like Adelle Davis, the woman who writes those health-through-diet books and who is charming, wise, smart, pleasant to look at and an expert in an interesting field.

With ten million people watching, with Johnny Carson endorsing, with over two hundred television stations showcasing, an appearance on the *Tonight Show* can make an act, move a book, sell out a play, start a cleanup drive or curtail American sex, all of which *Tonight* has done.

Because of this influence, the agents-managers-fixers-manipulators of the world will try anything to get whatever they're selling on display in studio 6-B.

Offered to the talent coordinators directly or indirectly, during the day or after hours, are cash, tickets, drinks, meals, trips, stock, vacations, participations, profit sharings, dope, and odd and assorted recreations, if their private inclinations run thusly.

That way lies only trouble—and an abruptly amputated career with the *Tonight Show*. The talent coordinators learn early that any special favors, bought or given, can mean their jobs at Raritan Enterprises, Inc., and probably throughout the broadcast world.

"If you're going to sell a guest spot on one of the shows, kid," Craig Tennis was advised when he first joined the show, "sell it for a quarter of a million dollars. That's probably what you'll need to live on when you get blackballed for life in this business."

The warning sank in. Today, he won't even accept or return phone calls from people who mention they could "slip him a little."

There was one famous case of payola. A talent coordinator received a telephone call one day from a man who said he owned the largest lobster in captivity. The producers and Carson thought it might make a short but funny interview.

The talent booker invited the man on the show and he arrived with a huge crate containing a lobster as large as a desk top. Man and lobster went on the show, visited with the host, talked out the problems of living with a giant lobster. ("What do you feed him, guests?" and "I'd hate to wrestle that one over a pot of boiling water" were some of the comments made on and behind the cameras.) When he was ushered off the stage, the man thanked the talent booker, put on his coat and was halfway out the door when a yell stopped him.

"Hey, your lobster. You forgot your lobster," the booker called.

"You can have him," the man shot back.

"Have him?"

"Sure, I don't need him any more. I just bought him tonight—after you said I could come on the show. I bought him down at the fish market."

A very large lobster and a very hungry group of talent coordinators repaired to one of their apartments, lit a fire, found a couple of pots large enough to boil the lobster. Just when it was properly steaming, it was time to watch that evening's show—which they had taped hours before.

They all settled down on the floor, plates full of steaming lobster in front of them, and ate it as they watched the very same lobster scurrying around the studio floor on camera two.

"Now there's an act you can get your teeth into," one of them said.

Tennis' greatest disappointment lies in the legend that his job must bring him packs of pretties to make his cold bachelor nights a bit warmer.

"I thought I'd have starlets, show girls, actresses, singers and those great-bodied acrobatic dancers all after my body for a chance," he said. "So far all I've had is the opportunity to baby-sit a starlet's three-year-old daughter while she appeared on the show."

Actually, Tennis shies away from pretty girls for the show.

"I don't know why it is," he says, "but beautiful girls tend to stop using their brains at a very young age. Someone—their parents, teachers, somebody—does them a disservice by raving about their beauty. Then the boy friends do it. Then the agents or the managers or the photographers or the press or the studios. By the time they get to us, their eyelashes are longer than their IQs. What we need are more Ali McGraws: beautiful, yes, but fascinating, too. What we get are Betty Boops."

Not all non-beauties are automatically desirable either. Tennis reads eight to ten new books a week—books sent to the *Tonight Show* offices by hopeful publishing houses. Out of those ten, Tennis says he may select one of two authors for an interview and, of those authors, perhaps one will get a free drink of scotch and a shove through the curtain into the fixed red eye of the *Tonight Show* cameras.

The show doesn't want or need too many serious authors, too many ecologists, educators, politicians or scientists.

"By eleven-thirty at night," goes the talent coordinator's golden rule, "the viewer has had two major newscasts plus bulletins to interrupt his television shows when and if necessary. The basic job of the *Tonight Show* is to entertain. If our ten million viewers thought we were going to do ninety minutes of man's inhumanity to man every night, they'd rather watch test patterns."

In essence this is what Carson and his directors and his producers have been preaching through the years. They watched Merv Griffin do the confrontations. They let Dick Cavett talk to the high domes. They saw David Frost attack, attack, attack. People turn to the *Tonight Show to* relax.

"If there is a confrontation on the *Tonight Show* it is not Gore Vidal and William Buckley yelling, 'You're another!' at each other live right here on our stage on cameras two and three," says Tennis. "It's more like Shelley Winters saying, 'I don't like your wife,' and David Susskind telling

Shelley she's fat. By the way, we'd like to replay that particular show and have had a lot of requests to do it. But neither Shelley nor David will give us permission.

"We try to run a balanced show at all times," he continues. "Should we do a full ninety minutes with Dr. Ehrlich [*The Population Bomb*] we know we won't get as high a rating as when we have Barbra Streisand. When we feel it important to have a Jim Garrison on we try to balance it that night or the next with a Buddy Hackett or a Jack Benny so we don't have a viewing disaster. Some people write and tell us we keep having the same people over and over, which is true for them. And others write and tell us they don't know nine out of ten of the guests we have on, which is true, too, for that group. I guess somewhere between is *our* truth."

Politicians can be a real problem. If they announce their candidacy or take sides on an issue, the *Tonight Show* is forced to give equal time to other candidates or spokesmen for the other sides. "Too much of this and we'd be the late, late news instead of the *Tonight Show*," Tennis says.

To keep things, you might say, upbeat, at least half of the guests booked on these shows do things musical. They sing—alone, in twos, threes, fours or squadrons; they dance —showing either a lot of leg or a lot of guts; and they squeeze musical notes out of tubing, wires or animal skins.

If the guest is known as a personality more than as a performer (Sammy Davis, Jr., Frank Sinatra) that person is picked out by Carson and his producers. However, if the guests' claim to fame is as Australia's Lilting Lassie or the Syncopation Sisters doing the Emancipation Proclamation on the theremin and jew's-harp, then the show music men get into the act—both in picking them and accompanying them through the show, physically and musically. All musical acts check in and are checked out with the musical director.

Through the years, being the *Tonight Show* musical director or one of its snide side men has carried its own form of fame. Milton DeLugg, Jose Melis, Skitch Henderson and Doc Severinsen were all assorted twangers, bangers, blowers or squeezers until late television brought them early recognition.

These are the men who have picked the musical acts:

Milton DeLugg, a composer, conductor and accordionist, was the musical director of *Broadway Open House* for both Jerry Lester and Morey Amsterdam. His quintet was called "DeLugg's Phony Philharmonic" and its main job was to supply drum rolls, rim shots, cymbal crashes and woodblock knocks for pratfalls and cat calls. In addition, it ground out old soft-shoe music for Lester's twinkling toes, and *on-tune* backgrounds for Amsterdam's counterpoint cello playing. In addition to conducting the music on *Broadway Open House*, DeLugg also worked with lyricists on songs he could introduce on that show. One of them, called "Orange Colored Sky," was exposed more on that show than Dagmar's chest. Both that chest and that song became national topics . . . on the tips of everyone's tongues. Verbally, of course.

Steve Allen was the only late night television host who was also a trained musician. As such, he depended less upon cut-and-dried "spot" appearances by guests and used music and musical performers as the spinal structure of his shows. He overshadowed his musical conductor, a fair-haired classical musician named Skitch Henderson. Allen's comedy monologues were done from a piano bench with assorted runs, trills and punchy melodies underlining the punch lines. His personal friendships with working musicians and performers enabled him to organize entire programs around two-beat Dixieland or cool jazz or the hard rock sound which was known then as Race-and-Blues Music. Allen also used late night television to showcase his bids for ASCAP immortality. The most noted—a song which has over a hundred different records and which became Allen's personal theme song—was "This Could Be the Start of Something. . . ." Today, Allen is listed in ASCAP as the writer of over three thousand songs, many of them created, composed and presented during Allen's *Tonight Show* period.

Another musician who ground out tunes like a hurdy-gurdy printout was Jose Melis. A graduate of the Havana, Cuba, Conservatory of Music and New York's Juilliard Graduate School, Melis found it's who you know in addition to what you know when he went job-hunting. Who he knew was Jack Paar. Melis had met Paar while they were both in the Army. His friendship with Paar was close enough so that he was invited to play Mendelssohn for Jack's wedding. It was inevitable that when Paar said, "I will," to NBC Melis should be invited along again to play the coupling refrain.

Using his Cuban accent for laughs and his piano for but-seriously-folks efforts, Melis tried again and again to come up with a *Jack Paar Show* version of "Orange-Colored Sky" or "This Could Be the Start," etc. Two of his songs, "I M 4 U" and "I Know What You Want," were both used as Paar show themes with little success. However, on New Year's Eve, 1958, he played a new tune called "Once in a Lifetime" which Decca Records got all excited about and rushed into record pressings. It turned out not to be Decca or Melis' once-in-a-lifetime hit. Years later, however, a melody with the same title from a Broadway show became second only to the "Maine Stein Song" for whiskey baritones all over the nation.

An Englishman, known sometimes as Lyle Cedric Henderson, sometimes as Skitch, and sometimes as a TV character named Sydney Ferguson, had as much to do with late night television music as the NBC chimes. Nobody outside of Pat Weaver or perhaps a peripatetic producer had more jobs with more late night shows than Henderson did. His most noted was as musical director with the *Johnny Carson Show*. There, he was teased, alternately, for his (a) blond beard, (b) British accent, (c) U-boat commander appearance. An extensively trained classical pianist, Henderson started his career conducting for M-G-M star Judy Garland and worked for that studio as a composer and arranger. Later, he was an accompanist for Bing Crosby and Frank Sinatra.

After World War II he landed a job on a radio program in Los Angeles. It featured another newcomer named Steve Allen. A few years later, he worked with Dave Garroway on a radio program and then on the *Garroway at Large* television show—the one which set so much of the relaxed, easygoing pattern of the later *Tonight Show*. In September 1954, Skitch Henderson became the musical director of Steve Allen's *Tonight Show* and a year later developed a bright-eyed idiot in a derby hat named Sydney Ferguson who was part of Allen's pack of laugh-getting "men-on-the-street." When Steve Allen left the *Tonight Show* spot for a Sunday night show, Skitch went with him.

Later, in June 1962, he returned to the *Tonight Show* but this time with a new host, Johnny Carson. Doubling in brass—musically and professionally—Skitch also worked as over-all musical director of NBC-TV and NBC radio. In late 1966, after a period of bickering and misunderstandings and hallway shootouts in the executive suites of 30 Rockefeller Plaza, Henderson told NBC that both he and his contract were running out at the end of September, and they did.

"He was always miscast," said one of the producers. "He wanted to play symphony hall music, we wanted him to play music hall tunes."

An upstairs executive said, "His idea of a show tune medley was Wagner's *Ring*."

Commented a third, "He wanted to do the NBC chimes with Fritz Reiner, the Royal Philharmonic and La Scala."

Scurrying about to find someone who understood more of what NBC and Carson stood for, the network executives and show producers reached into the archives and blew the dust off of Milton DeLugg.

Commenting on the selection, Carson said, "Milton is a

talented musician . . . he'll be a tremendous asset to the program."

Said DeLugg, "This . . . might be called the world's most delayed encore. . . ."

Between jobs on NBC's late night television shows, De-Lugg had written the music and lyrics for an animated film, worked as a side man in musical recording sessions, conducted TV series musical backgrounds and worked on recording dates with the likes of Dinah Shore and Soupy Sales.

A year later, DeLugg was out, and a fast-lipped wiseacre and trumpeter became the new musical conductor for Johnny Carson's combined three-ring ragadoo. His name was Carl "Doc" Severinsen and he had been with the *Tonight Show* musical group since Skitch Henderson lifted his first baton in an attempt to lift its taste. Carl was nicknamed "Doc" as in Little Doc because his father was Big Doc, an Arlington, Oregon, dentist.

Doing things with the mouth was a family trait, and Little Doc did his with a trumpet. When he was twelve he won a state band contest, and before he was eighteen he went on the road with Ted Fiorito's band. He played with Tommy Dorsey, Benny Goodman and on the Steve Allen and Dinah Shore shows before he became an NBC staff musician on the "swing shift" with Johnny Carson.

Where Skitch Henderson was teased for his beard and his tight-fitting, hacking-pocketed apparel, Severinsen earned his own reputation for mod clothing. One night he appeared on the show wearing a puce Pucci tie and Carson cracked, "I wouldn't wear that to fondle Randolph Scott's saddlehorn." Delighted with the uproarious audience reaction, the show's writers decided to make Doc's wardrobe part of his act. From impressionistic Pucci four-in-hands, they dressed him in crushed velvet knickers, rhinestone jumpsuits, suede and satin shirts, and tapestry cloaks. Each night, as surely as Ed McMahon said, "And now, h-e-e-e-r-e-e's

Johnnnnnneeeeee . . ." Johnny had something to say about Doc's apparel. With both Carson and Severinsen blowing Severinsen's horn, Little Doc has made almost the income he would have enjoyed as a dentist. At last count—by informed peekers—he was making over a half million dollars a year.

But the lure of that good old reliable, year-in-and-out ASCAP money for the man who can hit a musical hit remains as constant with the *Tonight Show* musical conductors as the show itself. DeLugg tried with "Orange-Colored Sky." Allen tried with "This Could Be the Start of Something Big," Melis tried with "Once in a Lifetime." And these days, one of the closing themes on the Johnny Carson *Tonight Show* is called "The Way I Feel About You." It was written by Doc Severinsen and associate music director Tommy Newsom. Each time it's played, the big piggy bank at ASCAP swallows another farthing or two for Doc's silver-threads-among-the-gold future days.

When the show was located in New York (it moved to California during May of 1972) the talent coordinators leaned toward New York-based celebrities, personalities and stars. There was a strong feeling that New York performers and thought leaders are more relaxed, easier to be with and better ad-libbers. California personalities, the talent searchers point out, are script-trained or used to having their agents talk for them. New York actors, for example, are always on and always on the street, hustling their careers. They meet and talk to people all day long in Manhattan. Californians are usually off, off with their clothes and off their diving boards. Every talent seeker on the show has had the sad experience of recommending a comedian who was brilliantly funny when he did his own material but sat like a stick when it came time to say "hello" to Johnny or any other unrehearsed line. In one case, even David Frost, on his show, was asked a question and hemmed and hawed and finally said, "I can't answer that. I have no material on the subject," one coordinator pointed out.

Is the show different when Carson isn't there? Do the talent people search as hard for the best-drawing guests?

"When a book, a movie, a play, or a politician needs promoting it's on their schedule, not on Johnny's," says one of the producers. "They can't hold up an opening night, a publishing date or an election because Johnny's not going to be on that night or that week. They come on when it's best for them and, of course, for us. Some of our substitute hosts ask for special guests to work with them, people they're comfortable with. We do our best to get them but the long-term commitments still stand.

"Yes, the audience is smaller when Carson isn't on a particular night, but, remember, even with a smaller viewership it's still greater than the other two late talk shows ever put together, combined."

One female magazine editor has been on the program several times, but never with Carson. "I don't believe there is a Johnny Carson," she says.

There are a lot of guests who might feel that way. One year Carson was off his seat seventy-seven days and guests who had looked forward to saying, "The way I see it, *Johnny,*" were saying, "The way I see it, *Orson, Jerry, Alan, Carl, Woody, Bill, Joe* or *Flip.*"

Getting on the show when Carson is on the show is hardest. Getting on with any of the *Tonight Show* hosts is very hard. Practically nobody gets on without an agent or a manager or a publisher or a spokesman of some type to get them into the first interview. Whole new companies like the one run by Tom Cassidy and Abbie Brown out of Boston have been set up purely to introduce tomorrow's talkers to the show personnel.

Besides taking telephone calls from sources they trust, the talent coordinators and producers also read the daily newspapers, weekly magazines and most newsworthy new books. They divide up the new movies in town and see them, call Celebrity Service every day to see who flew in, watch other talk shows to see who they are booking and spend many of their nights drinking Cokes in gloomy saloons looking for another Professor Irwin Corey, a Mort Sahl, a Bill Cosby, a Barbra Streisand.

Or let's say they were looking for and found—you.

They wanted you to be a guest on the *Tonight Show*.

What do you do? Where do you go? What would it be like?

The first place you go is to the special Raritan Enterprises *Tonight* offices at NBC in Burbank, California.

You would have an appointment, of course, with one of the talent bookers. While you were sitting in the waiting room, looking around at the pictures of Johnny sky diving, boxing with Muhammad Ali and flying with the Air Force Thunderbirds, you'd notice that the receptionist's desk is covered with mail, with packages, with crates, cartons and bags.

Some of it is mail asking for tickets, some of it is mail asking for Johnny Carson's picture, some of it is from people who want to be on the show to sell anything from a statue to a statute. Looking at the pile makes you realize how far you've come already.

The talent coordinator finally appears and takes you into a small cubicle where he (she) smiles, offers you coffee, picks up a lined pad and pencil and says, "Tell me about yourself."

He isn't being pleasant. He's camera-testing you right there. If you slump, fidget, puff nervously on a cigarette, slurp your coffee, whine, lisp, swear, pick your nose or develop a matched set of twitches, chances are you'll be escorted, very soon, to the outside door and told the show will "be in touch."

Of course, if you've come up with a cancer cure, the answer to lasting world peace, a three-hundred-mile-per-gallon carburetor, or the Presidency of the United States (or any country of over 10,000,000) the importance of having you on the show will outweigh that cute little habit you have of spitting as you talk.

But chances are you need the *Tonight Show* more than it needs you and getting to the talent coordinator is only the first test. If you looked interesting enough, sounded knowledgeable (or wacky) enough and seem to be the kind Carson can work with, the talent coordinator will probably tell you the day and date you might be on. If he needs an emergency replacement because tonight's guest thought he was supposed to be there tomorrow night and is still in Anchorage, be ready to go on. If you're just starting out on a cross-country tour to promote (a) a new religion, (b) a book, (c) a cosmetic line, (d) a movie, (e) or modular housing, the talent man may suggest that you go ahead and do your six-shows-a-day roundelay and then come back to them after you've been to San Francisco, Chicago, Seattle and "the Coasts" left or right. He and his chums feel that the more exposure you get on local shows the more comfortable you're going to be on Your Big Chance. And he's right. By the time most promotion-tour people hit the finish lap at the Carson show, they can not only come up with the answers but the questions too and tell the producers which ones get the biggest laughs, tears, gasps, sobs and encore requests.

Okay, the night you're to be on finally comes up. They want you at the studio an hour early, you keep telling yourself as you sit in the parking lot at Burbank two hours early. Well, you pacify yourself, there *could* have been a traffic jam on the Hollywood freeway.

They don't really want you to bring along your mother, your best friend, his wife, your writers, your agent, your editor, your tennis coach or Ferrari mechanic unless they're part of your act. The reason they don't want you to do that is because everybody else on the show that night will show up with one or more of the above to carry their scripts, their clothes or their flasks. These are the important-looking people who will be sitting in your chair or leaning against your table in the dressing room you are assigned to share with another "star." All of them will assume you're from the valet department at NBC and one will probably ask you to run out and get him paper cups and some ice.

Don't bother explaining who you are. They've never heard of you (even if you are the glittering star of the evening). At some point one of the wall drapers may even go out in the hall and ask someone if *you* aren't possibly in the wrong room.

Your talent coordinator will come by eventually and assure them that, yes, you are also on the show. He listens to the boy comic tell his routine about Wilt Chamberlain and Aristotle Onassis, which isn't too funny to you but which the talent man says he can use on the show. Then the co-ordinator gives you a copy of the "guide line" sheet which goes to Carson. It outlines what he will probably say to you and what you should probably say back to him.

You're suddenly shoved down the hall into a room filled with barber chairs, pots of Max Factor Pancake and make-up people so magnificently dressed, so cunningly barbered, so plucked, tweezed, glossed and lacquered that they make people like Zsa Zsa Gabor keep reassuring themselves that they are the fairest ones of all, even if it is somebody else's mirror.

This isn't their entire life. Working on certain shows, on split shifts, at odd hours, they all have outside interests. One owns a water bed factory and three retail stores. Another sells scuba gear. The third has a fried-chicken-stand franchise in south Glendale. He's the one who sponges your face with a muck of orange pancake and water. He dabs some white grease under your eyes to reflect the light away from the circles and bags, puts a heavier flesh color on those deep furrows you have between your nose and lips, swipes around your neck with the sponge, making sure that your collar gets a good half-inch blend of the color, tilts the chair forward and flips you out of it. During the entire two-minute beautification process, he has not once interrupted his description of the new five-speed, stereo-cartridged, six-cylindered, black-leathered, yellow-varnished, chrome-trimmed Porsche he's buying and what a bargain he got at only eighty-fiveninetyfiveninetyfive at a friendly, going-out-of-business dealership in the valley.

As you walk to the door, you notice a smaller room with one chair in it and a make-up man solicitously and patiently working on the occupant. It is Johnny Carson with a tissue towel around his neck and a glass of clear liquid (vodka?) in his hand. The only sound in that room is not the make-up man but a producer making soothing noises. Carson nods and the experienced make-up man's hand moves right along with the head.

As you leave the make-up room, the talent coordinator swoops you up and whisks you along the hall into a "greenroom." The greenroom is the traditional backstage room for actors waiting to go on stage or television shows. If nobody looks important, don't be fooled. They *may* only be agents or relatives of the other guests on the show but they may not. One night a minor author waiting to go on loudly shushed three people seated near him. They were talking and he was trying to watch the show on the television monitor in the room. The people he told to shut up turned out to be Mimi Benzell, Beverly Sills and Rudolph Bing of the Metropolitan Opera company who were also waiting to go on.

The greenroom has chairs, sofas, the television monitor, a large hot pot of coffee, some cakes and the smell of fear.

Hundreds, thousands, of people waiting to go on the *Tonight Show* have left the stink of nervousness in the furnishings. It permeates the vinyl couch covers, the heavily woven drapes, the thick carpeting. Twenty-four-hour deodorants wear out in twenty-four seconds around here. Large beads of perspiration pop out on faces. Collars suddenly get tight. One lady gets up and just paces, back and forth, back and forth. A man dips quickly into his pocket for a silver flask which he flips to his mouth for a fast gargle. In the corner is one calm, smiling performer. The combination of three Librium and three martinis has finally worked on him. If he timed it right he'll get on, do his stuff and get off before that combination puts him away for the night.

If you didn't bring your own nerve tonic, the show has a supply. There is a special bar set up for guests (*Warning: Any member of the crew touching this bar will be dismissed from the show*) and it has a half bottle of vodka, a three-quarters-full bottle of scotch, some water and an ice bucket that's hardly touched. This is panic drinking time. Very few bother with the niceties of ice or muddlers. One of the talent watcher's jobs is to make sure the guests don't get whiskey and water on the brain. It is an ailment which is contagious at these talk shows and which usually doesn't show up until the guest either tries to enter and stumbles over his feet or tries to talk and stumbles over his mouth.

It doesn't help at all when the talent coordinator turns to you, smiles nicely and says, "Do your best. Remember ten million people are watching."

And you know, just know, that out there in that ten million are the people you live with and your mailman, old teachers, secretaries, bowling friends and all the enemies you ever made in your life just waiting for you to prove what they've said all along, that you're an idiot.

The *Tonight Show* is taped at dinnertime for its hour-and-a-half length. Once started, the show is done straight through, just as though it was live television. Nobody is going to yell, "Stop the cameras," if you say something wrong, drool down your chin or even swear. The swear words will be bleeped out by the NBC censor, the drool they will leave there because the director had the camera on Johnny and not on you at the time (which is very likely) and the wrong information you gave out you'll just have to correct by backtracking and wimbling your way around it.

One of the early decisions you're going to have to make is

whether you're going on the *Tonight Show* once or if you'd like to be asked back. If you're convinced it's your one big chance, plug whatever you're selling whenever you can. Carson or the producer may call for a commercial to cut you off but then again they may not. You play the odds on their mood of the moment.

Ladies selling cosmetics seem to get their feet in their mouths trying to get a foot in America's door. Jinx Falkenburg, an ex-model, once came on the show to hawk her beauty aides. Every time Carson tried to get her onto another, more interesting subject, she'd bring it right back to her sample kit. She managed to cut out any interesting conversation for eight minutes but she also managed to cut herself off of the come-back-soon list, too.

Zsa Zsa Gabor was handled differently one night by the producers. She was rambling on at great and boring length about *her* line of cosmetics, and the producers finally clipped her spiel by cutting in a sudden commercial for another famous line of cosmetics.

If you want to be asked back, let the show do the plugging of your wares and you sell yourself. The charming guests— the Drs. Stillman and Reuben, the Erich Segals, the Irving Wallaces—are asked back again and again because they have become entertainers and not book salesmen. If you're selling a book, Carson may hold it up, or cameras may cut away to the cover. To the *Tonight Show* producers that's considered enough of a plug. Now it's your turn to be the charming, winsome, fascinating person the talent coordinator found you to be during the initial interview.

Carson will stick pretty close to the "guide line" questions the talent person gave you earlier. And he will expect you to come back with the answers, as written. Should he stray away from the outline, it is a compliment to you and he feels you can handle the conversation without a script prop. However, if you stray away from the subject he will feel you have pulled a fast one on him and he is unprepared for such tricks tonight and he will pull a commercial right across your face just like that and when it's gone you will be, too, and the chair will be filled with someone else.

Suddenly the show will be over and everybody will be waving at the cameras one minute and then the red lights on top of them will flame out and a voice will yell, "That's a wrap," or something like it and everyone will have a place to head for except you.

Even though this has been one of the headiest nights of your life and the glands are pumping high-test adrenalin into your motor centers, and you're now so exhilarated you can tell all the stories you didn't get to do on the show and you are even entertaining the idea of starting your own talk show, nobody is going to invite you to an after-show party. Remember, these people do this every night. They are tired. They have worked hard today. They still have to clean up, to repair or prepare work to do for tomorrow. And they have homes to go to, also.

You can either go back to the dressing room you share with the comic and his crew (the "Wilt-Ari" joke flopped, you noted with satisfaction) or you can keep the orange mask on and take it off later at home. Most men, heading for a drink after the show, remove it first. The Los Angeles vice squad still tends to sidle up to men in heavy make-up.

Except for the fact that Johnny, who you hadn't seen until air time, looked older (younger, grayer, sadder, wiser, happier, sexier—pick one or more) than he does on your television set, there will be one other surprise.

Now that ten million people have seen you on the air, you expect to be mobbed by people who recognize you instantly.

Nobody will (providing you are not an ax murderer, the President of the United States or Howard Hughes).

It is a proven fact that a person can go on the *Tonight Show*, sit there and *shmoos* for twenty minutes with the camera right on his face the whole time, then go about his business for a week or more before even his best friend says, "Say, didn't I see you on the Johnny Carson show?"

By some trick of the American memory, the longer the time between the show and the encounter, the more people will remember you. A year after your appearance, a stranger on the street or at a party will quote something you said on the show. But never the day after, never.

But you are not alone in this.

It is reported that people still stop Jack Paar on the street and say they enjoyed him on the *Tonight Show* last night . . . some ten years after he left it.

☆ **12**

It certainly looks simple enough.

All it takes is an hour and a half a night, some color cameras, a guy who shoots from the lip, and four or five talkers who get $290 apiece for being the major part of the show. In return for this, the rewards can run twenty-eight, twenty-nine, even thirty million dollars a year.

That's the way they kept thinking at the Columbia Broadcasting System and the American Broadcasting Company. They looked over NBC's late night station line-up (more than two hundred twenty-five), at how many television-equipped homes they reached (more than ninety-nine percent), and what the network got for a commercial (close to twenty thousand dollars) and how many they ran in each program (nine). Even with large discounts to the big advertisers, a kickback of money to the stations for the use of the hall, and handing

Raritan Enterprises, Inc., six or six and a half million dollars a year, they knew that NBC's *Tonight Show* was not only the rating master of the late night television hours but that it was NBC's—or maybe the entire industry's—biggest single money-maker, too.

"There must be a buck in there somewhere for *us*," they said.

And there is. Carson's *Tonight Show* plays to about thirty-five percent of all people watching late night television. That means two out of three homes are still available and so is one out of every two television advertising dollars spent late at night.

Long-faced men carrying long lists of numbers call men carrying long lists of names into rooms with long conference tables.

"I see Carson's got new ratings, new stations and new sponsors," they say. "Our affiliate in south Texas just switched to NBC so they could get the show. One sponsor just left our late movies for Carson, and his ratings have gone up three points this week."

"Don't worry, Chief, we've got the answer," someone shoots back.

They haven't. Or at least they haven't found it in Carson's first ten years on the *Tonight Show*.

Lord knows they've tried. Lord knows it looked easy enough.

After all, how tough can a talk-variety show be?

How tough? Ask Joey Bishop. Ask Merv Griffin. Ask Dick Cavett how tough it is to go up against the midnight magic of the NBC *Tonight Show*.

The other networks thought these men would be part of the answer. Instead, they became part of the problem. Back before them, CBS and ABC had depended upon their late shows and movies to get big-number audiences during the waning hours. What they refused to notice was that Carson could pick them off any time he wanted to with an extra super celebrity or a news-making confrontation. It was rare that a showing of *The Incredible Shrinking Man* could set up an incredible shrinking tune-in for Carson.

Too, the supply of motion pictures good enough to keep people away from the *Tonight Show* was limited. Some of the better ones were so overexposed they were played up to seventy times in a city.

In 1967 the American Broadcasting Company picked Joey Bishop, a raspy-mannered saloon cutup, to help themselves cut up the midnight money. Bishop was what Jack Paar called a "Joey-Jerry" comic, the kind with jokes about South Philadelphia, about Mah-Jongg, about lox and Las Vegas and Miami Beach hotels. He weighed, it was reported as a press item of interest, only two pounds, fourteen ounces at birth and, one NBC man said, "never became any more of a heavyweight than that."

For his opening night, NBC sent flowers and, sensing an early death, Bishop publicly thanked them for "making the arrangements."

Bishop, who had sat in for Carson during his vacations, was a lot smarter than ABC. He knew that the network was putting him on against a proven killer. He felt he needed strength and security and he asked for some of Jack Paar's ex-staff to help him produce the show. He also asked for a firm thirty-nine-week contract because he knew miracles seldom happen but never on one thirteen-week cycle. And he asked for a freshly upholstered battleground and ABC spent two million dollars fixing up new color studios for him on Vine Street in Hollywood.

On opening night he came out, said his announcer's name was Regis Philbin and that was "the Latin name for Hugh Downs." He sat in a duplicate of the *Tonight Show* set and welcomed Debbie Reynolds, Danny Thomas, a "new discovery" named Brenda Arnau and Governor of California Ronald Reagan, who welcomed him and the show to that state.

Bishop had it all his own way that night. Carson was still off the air waiting for NBC to make it an additional even round million to bring him around. Asked if he would come back in time to blunt Bishop's opening show, Carson said, "It wouldn't be fair . . . wouldn't look good for me. It would just look like a publicity stunt."

When Carson did check into his *Tonight Show* one week later, he left ABC officials sitting there looking at thirty-eight guaranteed but seemingly all downhill weeks ahead of them. Bishop's golden hours had lasted one week. He never captured the audience size or enthusiasm that ABC had gambled on owning.

The first night back, Carson bounced on, laughed a lot, even lifted Bishop's Jewish jokes. "I really feel guilty working at Passover," he said. "You know, you're supposed to eat unleavened bread and I came back for more dough."

Talking about his walkout and return, he said, "I received a nice note from NBC-TV President Don Durgin. I would have felt better if he hadn't written it on the back of an eight-by-ten glossy of Bob Newhart."

Meanwhile, over at ABC, Bishop had asked Jack Paar to come on his show and help double-team Carson's return. The theory was that Paar had been off the show longer, therefore should get even more of the curious to tune in.

It didn't work. The *Tonight Show* pulled its regulars plus the people curious to see Johnny's return and ended up with forty percent of the audience. The hit-'em-high-hit-'em-low team of Bishop and Paar had to settle for twelve percent.

CBS stood by for two years, hoping Carson and Bishop would knock each other off. One out of five late night viewers were watching Bishop. One out of three were watching Johnny Carson. The other forty-seven percent were fair game.

Up until the late summer of 1969, CBS-owned stations and affiliates had continued to show movies in those late hours. The CBS network was getting nothing out of this. Meanwhile, NBC was making twenty-six million a year from

Tonight and ABC, even with its poor second position, was attracting eleven million dollars for Bishop. The CBS numbers men figured that there was still another twelve or thirteen million dollars that could be drained out of the Lever Brothers, the Colgates and Bristol-Myers and that it belonged, by rights of salvage, to CBS.

CBS finally decided to make it a three-way fight for the eighteen million viewers who were watching late night television.

To hoe their row, they picked a farm hand named Merv Griffin. Griffin had been a singer with the ultra-square Freddy Martin band and his recording of "I've Got a Lovely Bunch of Coconuts" had sold a million records. That isn't why CBS picked him, however. Griffin had done a nice job sitting in for Paar and Carson during their absences and had even been in the final balloting at NBC headquarters when they picked Carson to replace Paar. In the middle sixties, Griffin had sold his own idea of a talk show to the hustling Westinghouse network and in five years their salesmen placed it on one hundred forty-two stations.

With one eye, Griffin could see the problems that Bishop was having but the other eye noticed how much money Carson was making. "You can do it, kid," his advisers said. Sure he could—Griffin asked for somewhere between ten and twenty thousand a week, for a six-year contract and for two million dollars' worth of clean-up-paint-up-fix-up of a New York theatre he decided was more comfy than a studio.

Not all of the CBS executives were shouting Merv with verve. The wiser heads pointed out that Griffin's syndicated Westinghouse show was mostly successful in daytime hours. They dragged out studies of the tragedies that happened when a few stations tried to pit Griffin against Carson and Bishop at night.

"All the public needs to love him is to know him," one promotion executive countered. "Let's spend two or three million to familiarize him to them." They spent it on advertising. It might have been better to send a dollar each to that many people.

Griffin went on a hundred yards behind Bishop and a mile behind Carson. More than one hundred ninety stations were carrying the *Tonight Show* then, more than one hundred sixty were carrying Bishop, and the best that mighty CBS could come up with was one hundred fifty of their stations to beam the first *Merv Griffin Shows*. They had hoped to start with more than two hundred but many of the holdouts still had libraries of expensive films they had to play more often to recover their investments.

Meanwhile, the *Joey Bishop Show* was starting to limp along in that three-way race. Bishop's buddy, Regis Philbin, believed that what was good for Paar and Carson might be good for him and he walked off the show one night, complaining that CBS had never really wanted him. "I'm not Ed McMahon," he said, which came as no great revelation to the cast, the crew or the audience that night. Nobody ran after him because nobody was sure how long the entire show was going to be around.

Just as Jack Paar had taken over the *Joey Bishop Show* the night Johnny Carson returned to NBC, so other guests began taking over. One time two of Bishop's guests began a heated discussion across him and wouldn't stop. Finally, trying to get back in control, the host cracked weakly, "From turning my neck so much I think I've worn out my shirt."

Bishop believed it was the way to play the game. "If I have a NASA scientist or a Billy Graham, I can't become a scientist myself or become religious," he said. "The only thing for me to do is play my stupidity against their knowledge."

It was probably not the thing to do. Viewers began clicking their dials to the *Tonight Show*.

Late in 1969, ABC decided to replace Bishop with a show host who could read books without moving his lips. His name was Dick Cavett. Cavett had been around late night tele-

vision ever since Jack Paar. He had worked on the *Tonight
Show* as a junior writer (called a Talent Coordinator so they
could pay him less) and then later as a fully titled and
salaried show writer. When Carson took over, Cavett stayed
on, writing sometimes for Carson and sometimes for himself. He finally talked the producers and Carson into letting
him try his own jokes out of his own mouth and the television
audience was taken by the shy-appearing, boyish comedian.

With his background of what worked and what didn't in
late night television, Cavett decided to create his own type
of show. He had no plans to do a Las Vegas lounge side
show like Joey Bishop. He had no eagerness to be the guest-
zinging pixie like Carson. Instead, he sat down with dome-
heads like anti-war spokesman and Harvard biologist Dr.
George Wald and journalist I. F. Stone. He talked at and
listened to Townsend Hoopes, author of a book about Lyndon
Johnson's Vietnam policies. And for a change of pace he
invited people like Jimmy "The Greek" Snyder, the Las Vegas
gambler who sets up betting odds on sports events. Although
Cavett does his homework, sported a 136 IQ (This was played
down so the audience wouldn't be afraid that it's an "intellectual" show). He probed, questioned, dug and wasn't afraid
to come out with a personal attitude or opinion. One time
when he found out that Oakland Raider quarterback Daryle
Lamonica's ambitions included killing all of Africa's "big
five" wild animals, he said he was glad other football teams
mistreated his guest.

Cavett's show was a true talk show because there was talk
and not interviews. Cavett spoke. He listened. He nodded.
He added or asked for an explanation. He created a literate
show, a cultural show, and a show that was amazingly interesting because of his attitudes and opinions and what he
managed to pull out of his guests.

One night former Georgia Governor Lester Maddox stood
up and walked off the show after a faceoff with ex-football
star Jim Brown. Another night Cavett put male chauvinist

writer Norman Mailer against femme lib leaders and, disturbed by the way Mailer was acting, even took sides with the ladies by picking up his chair and moving to their side of the stage. Many of the people barred by NBC from the *Tonight Show* were more than welcome on the *Dick Cavett Show*, providing, of course, he could get the blessings of the network. He was excited by the idea of natural, spontaneous guerrilla theatre and wanted to be in the thick of it.

Over at NBC, Carson's producers don't believe in face-to-face confrontations. They feel that, regardless of subject, there are millions of people out in television land who couldn't care less about it and who will turn away from the entire show. They're convinced that a nice song confronted by a pretty girl singer is about as much controversy as their audience wants.

"Let Cavett have that piece of the audience that calls itself intellectual," one of them said. "They wouldn't watch us anyway."

Most of the people producing the Cavett show were once part of the Johnny Carson show. In many of the shows they did with Cavett, they were working out years of frustrated ideas turned down by Carson or one of his producers as "too thinky" for that show.

Although Cavett and Carson may have had the same people on their shows—the Sammy Davis, Jrs., Zsa Zsa Gabors, Rex Reeds—they handled them differently. On the *Tonight Show*, Rex Reed would be encouraged to gossip about movie personalities he has profiled for magazines. On Cavett's program he was invited to talk about the death of the giant studios, the new-wave film makers, and the symbolism of Fellini.

But neither Dick Cavett's nor Merv Griffin's shows were what the trade papers call boffo box office.

At the end of the critical year 1970, Griffin's show had 3,370,000 viewers in late December, Cavett had 1,560,000, and Carson had 5,560,000.

It provided what NBC was saying, that *Tonight* out-pulled the other two late shows combined. It also cast in bronze the attitude of the *Tonight Show* producer when he said, "People don't want to think at the end of the day. They want to be entertained. We don't put on anything that's going to disturb them too much."

If people want to be disturbed late, late at night (once a week), they can always hook up with the *David Susskind Show*. One of the very first talk formats, the Susskind confrontations are seen in four dozen cities. Susskind's original presentations were celebrity talk shows but Susskind began to notice that after it got past the names and the credits there wasn't anybody at home. For a show that depended upon good, stimulating talk for survival, that was disastrous. He changed styles and began producing some of the strongest confrontations ever aired. He had telephone company officials come on to defend themselves against victims of bad service. He had black militants and white racists face each other down. He had winos and alcoholic abuse people at each other's habits. He's put the atheist and the priest, the pacifist and the soldier, even the smoker and the cancer surgeon in the same pit and let them paw at the dirt and at each other.

"It's great television," he has said, "great theatre in the home. It's the type of exciting television people deserve but aren't getting."

"It isn't at all," said a detractor, "he just lets people ramble dully along."

In early 1972, because of disappointing ratings and a dwindling list of sponsors, Merv Griffin was dropped by the CBS network and was picked up immediately by Metromedia to sell city by city to those stations wanting it. Producer of the show, ex-Paar and Carson writer Walter Kempley said, "We couldn't keep up our ratings because Carson had so many more stations than we did. City for city, though, we were right up there with *Tonight*."

As a farewell gesture, Griffin showed why he was going off.

On his last CBS show he told the audience highlights of his two and a half years with CBS. They weren't very exciting. There was the night Zsa Zsa Gabor and her jewels met jewel thief Willie Sutton. The whee of a night David Eisenhower came on. And the night the president of CBS ordered Abbie Hoffman cut out of an entire ninety-minute show because he was wearing an American-flag shirt.

Roger Miller sang his old song hit, "King of the Road," actor Joe Flynn said he had to pay to use the men's room at CBS now that the show was canceled, and Pamela Mason said she fed spaghetti Alfredo to wild raccoons in Hollywood. Griffin introduced the cue-card boy on camera and, faced with his big show-business opportunity, the youngster decided to tell a joke that started, "There were once two Jews . . ." "That's a Milton Berle story," said somebody, shoving him back behind the cameras again. "Good-by to the big eye [the CBS symbol]," they all said and CBS was back in the what-do-we-do-next business.

Although CBS went right back to late night movies, there remained a group of programming executives there who were assigned the awesome responsibility of dreaming up another late night talk/variety/make-money show.

This kind of show must start with the host. CBS began looking in the daylight. That's when they breed.

One host who had come up fast because of a way with words and people was a very young Englishman named David Frost. He comes on, heavily prepared research on hand and in his head, and probes, pokes, psychs, and scratches out the answers he wants. Most of his guests tend to admit interesting insights under Frost's continual scrabbling at them but eventually even the most fascinating dwindle into clichés and stories they've told on other programs. Frost tries to ferret out the sensational to top his one big claim to fame; he drove Arthur Godfrey to admit he'd had a vasectomy. It wasn't enough. Frost's show has been frozen out as a current offering.

Another day tripper is a man who looks like Merv Griffin, sings like Merv Griffin and is the operator of a syndicated show like Merv Griffin's. His name is Mike Douglas and many people mix up the two hosts and the two programs, as well as the interchangeable guests. The Douglas show, out of the Westinghouse network, is ten years old and on a hundred and fifty stations. It's main thrust is light fun, fun, fun. Keeping it light and happy is the dark and heavy order of the day.

"It's one of those shows the housewife doesn't watch," said one advertising agency media expert. "She turns it on the TV but continues walking around the house doing her chores. She can hear it and she doesn't miss anything. It's what Godfrey used to be on radio but not quite."

Although the show will book someone with good advance press like sexist writer Helen Gurley Brown, nothing interesting ever happens between the foaming cleanser commercials.

Another show proprietor who scuttles out in the daytime is Virginia Graham. After almost a decade on a show called *Girl Talk*, she put together her own answer for America's lonely housewives. The show runs to guests who tell how to make tissue paper flowers, or why the viewers should join the female liberation movement, or how to make a séance in your basement rumpus room in your spare time.

The ever industrious Dinah Shore has a show that gets all over the country by staying in the kitchen. It is not exactly a talk show. It is not exactly a cooking show. It is a show that books interesting guests who must, somehow, be involved with foods or recipes or cooking. This rigid and unexplainable limitation leads to such opening guest lines as, "You know, Dinah, you can't make a good cake without a good batter and, speaking of good batters, did I ever tell you about the time I hit two home runs in the World Series?" Or, "Dinah, let me show you the way Otto Preminger salted his food the night he took me to dinner and asked me to star in his forthcoming drama of intrigue, suspense and romance called . . ."

There are other talk-type shows. There are the local *show-meisters*: Ralph Story in Los Angeles, Bob Kennedy in Chicago, Joe Franklin in New York.

Dave Garroway is available.

Steve Allen is still doing his indestructible, funny syndicated show and it could go network within weeks within reason.

Jack Paar says he'll never go back to it but he's sitting there in Bronxville and he's been known to make snappy comebacks. He went on the Dick Cavett show one night to ask America to keep watching it. The plea might have worked but America wasn't watching *that* night either.

The old redhead, "Artha" Godfrey, showed up last year doing automobile commercials. If he can take on cars, why can't he take on Carson?

How about ABC's knowitall sports announcer, Howard Cosell? The very funny comedy writer, Carl Reiner? Orson Welles? Lauren Bacall? Bill Cosby? Even Richard Burton and Elizabeth Taylor transferring Get the Guest from *Who's Afraid of Virginia Woolf?* to Who's Afraid of Johnny Carson?

But then again, maybe there is no opportunity after all.

Perhaps there is no farm team of new "Here's Johnny's" for the same reason there are no new blacksmiths. The late night sit-sat-chit-chat kind of television may be headed thataway along with *Howdy Doody, Hopalong Cassidy* and *Omnibus.*

Before getting into another one of those CBS WEB INKS $10 MIL PACT *Variety* stories about another attempt to knock Carson off, some questions should be asked.

Are people going to switch channels from NBC to another to see, once again, Richard Boone's pockmarks, Jack Lemmon's capped teeth, Jerry Quarry's cauliflower ear, Lou Rawls' tonsils, Gwen Verdon's legs and Erich Segal's ambitions?

How many more times do they want to hear about Cleveland Amory's seals, Bill Cosby's scooter, George Jessel's bar mitzvah, Burt Reynolds' center fold, Henny Youngman's wife or whether either Brook Benton or Dr. Newton K. Wesley is opening a split week at the Desert Inn on March 3? How many more, O Lord, priests leaving their churches, Americans leaving their country, actresses leaving their studios, animal acts leaving their leavings?

How much more talk, talk, talk, talk, talk, without saying anything?

One time, when Jack Paar was hosting the *Tonight Show,* Joey Bishop was introduced, walked out, said, "Good evening," and sat down.

"Is that all you're going to say?" asked Paar.

"For $320, that's plenty," said Bishop.

It was the finest minute in twenty years.

☆ **13**

In the last year the nineteen-inch rectangular picture has changed.

It seems like one night the country was up to its bedsprings in . . . "yes, the critics loved it but Walter Kerr didn't . . . American men let American women push them around too much . . . my new series went on opposite the World Series . . . I recorded it with Peggy Lee . . . in my new Doubleday-published $5.95 book . . . so I said, 'I have a few minutes to make an ass of myself but you have all evening' . . . a split week in Tahoe, a month at the Blue Angel, then back to L.A."

And the next night a lot of the talkers had a gag *on* instead of in their mouths.

It was getting late for late night television.

Merv and Joey and Dick and Johnny had been running

four hundred guests a week past their cameras. Here he is, folks, watch him talk and there he goes, folks. Who's next?

"It opens at Radio City on the twenty-third."

"As Jack Lemmon was saying to me the other night . . ."

"My first break was at Grossinger's."

"That was the night my costume fell off."

"We'll be right back after this message."

But most of them didn't come back. For a while there, television viewers could get Merv's *Tonight Show*, Dick's *Tonight Show*, Joey's *Tonight Show* and the *Tonight Tonight Show*.

The original.

An original art form written, directed and produced for television.

Nobody in radio ever gambled ninety minutes of air time on an unscripted show with unrehearsed guests. The insanity of having people just talk at each other never struck the operators of vaudeville houses, circuses, state fairs or American Legion halls.

NBC's early television genius, Pat Weaver, dreamed that late night talk shows could make mass man into class man . . . the common man into the uncommon man.

But the common late night talk show did not become the uncommon one.

Merv, Joey and others had their picture tubes turned to the wall.

Even Dick Cavett's different kind of light dimmed through the talk show twilight.

"We killed the talk shows with talk," said one out-of-work producer of them. "We all tried to copy Carson and the *Tonight Show* because that's where the audience was and that's where the advertisers were and that's what my network wanted from me. Well, there's only one *Tonight Show* and when that's gone there'll never be anything like it again. And it's going, you mark my words," he finished.

"The real trouble," added one of the writers who worked

for him, "is that we were using people who could talk, yes, but who had nothing to say. How long could that be a winning combination?"

He was right, of course.

For millions of viewers, the idea of having Bob and Ray, Ann Elder, Ryan O'Neal, Rocky Graziano and Joseph Mankiewicz right there in the bedroom with them was heady stuff. They told fascinating stories about Sam Goldwyn, about Clark Gable, about the mythical night Noel Coward and Cole Porter and George Gershwin all played the piano and sang, together!

And it was not only the beautiful people who came to call, but it was the up-and-doers who dropped by to sit on the bed and chat away until sleep came. They were producing plays and writing best sellers and making films and hitting a ball and pulling a million dollars and stories out of their guitars, books, paintbrushes, tap shoes, pianos, lawbooks, universities, concert tours, blueprints, tankers, touring companies, fast food franchises, corporation spinoffs and two weeks at the Copa, four at the Fountainebleau, one at Loew's Strand.

And they were right there in the house, in the bedroom, for God's sake, these glorious, glamorous faces trying to entertain, trying to amuse, trying to impress, to get the watcher to like them and enjoy their stay. It was a thousand times better than going to even the best Hollywood party because, there, the viewer would be asked eventually to say something equally knowing about Harry Cohn's days at Columbia or "Lenny's" new symphony-mass or mess. This way, they didn't have to warm up the coffee, thaw out the danish or open the Hennessy. They didn't even have to shave or roll the curlers down to hear about going on location and rough cuts and "Doc" Simon's new play and the night David (Merrick or Susskind) came backstage at the show.

At first and for many years—five? ten? twenty?—this kind of there's-no-talk-like-show-talk hypnotized the nation's sleepless millions into believing they were part of a gay, amusing, illuminating, glamorous conversation.

Only here and there, now and then, did somebody point to the all-star, all-mouth review on the tube and say, "But show business has no clothes on."

"Hush," others would say, "that's a glamorous person and we are lucky to be allowed to listen in."

But eventually more and more noticed that their friends at the office, their bowling chums, their gas station mechanics, and the girl behind the Howard Johnson's counter were also talking and their conversations had nothing to do with Otto Preminger or two weeks at the Sands or Bobby Short but were about the people they knew, the street they lived on, the taxes they paid. And when that happened, television sets all over the country were tuned to one last, that is the first, of the talk shows or they clicked off right after the late night news.

"I'm surprised the audience interest lasted as long as it did," that out-of-work producer added. "It was always based on the suspicious notion that if people are good in a scripted show they would be good on an ad-lib one. Not outside of the *Second City* group they're not.

"It also assumed that show-business people who seem fast on their feet—and with their mouths—are. They aren't," the writer added. "Some of the biggest names in the business make fools of themselves when they get off the subjects of Palm Springs or the William Morris agency. It didn't take people long to see that."

Viewers could see that, sure, and they could also see that what had started out as a Super Communications idea—bright, knowledgeable people sharing ideas with each other—had turned into a bunch of fragmented monologues interrupted by a message from the host, the sponsor or another guest who thought he had been ignored long enough.

"As I was pointing out," one would point out.

"Let me add to what you are saying . . ." another would add.

"What you forget to mention," a third would mention.

"We'll be right back after this word," said the host.

There was little communication going on these last five years—with Carson, with Griffin, with Bishop. Guests had truly talked to each other on the Jack Paar show and they had even listened to each other. They listened so hard that every fortnight or so somebody would threaten to punch another guest right in the nose. But in late night's late history, guests came on only to do eight minutes of their own shill: the new movie, the Miami Beach date, the book, the vaccine, the mutual fund. They would simper and giggle and stack the clichés, metaphor after metaphor, atop one another until the whole show, and its audience, became one enormous ninety-minute yawn.

Talk show producers believed that there was nothing more frightening than an unexpected sound in the night. Like the front door squeaking open or a fire siren, or a scream, or a late night television show guest saying something startling, disturbing or important.

There is a gentleman's agreement on the *Tonight Show*, for example, that a guest employed in film work will plug a new picture or go for a stroll down memory lane with old ones, but will never mention the theories of Eisenstein, the limitations of the 10:1 Zoomar lens, or the hidden sexuality in Bergman's celluloid.

The current producer's theory continues to be that the twenty million insomniacs in front of thirteen million television sets do not want to hear Abbie Hoffman's side of the story or why our infant mortality rate is so bad or about Asian politics or how the syndicate is taking over Wall Street or how much mercury laces each tuna sandwich these days.

Instead, he fills $20,000-a-minute time—and millions of heads—with the wit of Zsa Zsa Gabor ("I think a girl should find love: I think she should marry and marry until she finds it"). And the wisdom of Sammy Davis ("Love your brother, man, that's all we got").

Most of the non-theatrical guests—the authors, the scientists, the politicians, the educators—are chosen not because of what they have to say but because of the way they look when they say it.

"Sure," said one booker, "we lean toward a good-looking physicist who can talk over a guy who is slow and hesitates —even if his discovery isn't as important."

It has reached the stage where a man who makes musical toilet paper holders and who has five funny stories about them can get eighteen minutes on the *Tonight Show* but a sewage engineer who is trying to save the country's drinking water can only get eight minutes or maybe none at all.

"The reason for that," according to the *Tonight Show* producers, "is because viewers have been shoved, jostled, insulted, robbed, unappreciated and unloved all day long. What they need—and want—is a little comfort like a pretty girl singing to them and a little relaxation like a few jokes, to take the raw edges off their nerves.

"The thinkers, the second-guessers, the sidelines players say we should turn our programs over to discussions of the Mideast crisis, or school busing problems, or the decay in our prisons or the insanities in our asylums. The people who suggest this should be put away themselves. Hell, ninety minutes of enlightened discourse on national unemployment wouldn't help the problem but only add to it—by adding our employee list to the unemployment lines."

Viewers (you, your wife, sister, mother, neighbors?) can't be bothered with Red Chinese firebombs but want Las Vegas fireballs instead. What you want, according to them, are Dick Shawn, Dayton Allen, Totie Fields, Phyllis Diller, Shecky Greene, Louis Nye, Karen Valentine, Lenny Kent, Copa-Fontainebleau-Riviera, Radio City on the twenty-third.

When the Dick Cavett show received its one-year suspended suspension in 1971, it was "because we were trying to do something important and meaningful and significant and worth while on each show," said one of the associate producers.

The Cavett show went from rambling, involved gabfests to snarling confrontations, odd-lot mixtures of personalities, brazen questionings and first-time-ever exhibitions just short of on-camera performances by four Masters and Johnson sex clinic volunteers, backed by the Mormon Tabernacle Choir.

It wasn't enough—on ABC's *Tonight Show*, NBC's *Tonight Show*, CBS's *Tonight Show*, or the Independent's *Tonight*—for a man to have cured hiccups, war, overpopulation, sickle cell anemia, or nail biting unless he could do six Rockette routines or a split week at the Playboy Club in Cleveland.

"If people wanted *Meet the Press, Issues and Answers* and *Face the Nation* at midnight, that's what we'd give them," said one CBS vice-president. "What they want is the supper show at the Sands and that's what they get."

"Not true," says one of the NBC spokesmen. "The *Tonight Show* has given valuable, important time to politicians, astronauts, scientists, teachers, medical men and other important people.

"We reach more people with more educational and serious messages than all of educational television. After all, you could have guests talk all day on educational television and not reach the audience we can give them in one minute."

Therein, the success and the failure of all late night talk shows and the *Tonight Show* and late night television.

Pat Weaver dreamed that television would take man to other planets, to the surgical operating room, to new dimensions in thought and social conscience.

The *Tonight Show* has exhibited the astronauts and their planetary films, the surgeons and their medical advances, the metaphysicians and the teachers and the politicians and their tranquillity-through-me theories. The common man walked the moon, stalked the virus, zipped open the inscrutable Eastern karmas to see if, with a little tailoring here and there, they might fit.

Except for a few people who disturb the public's taste as to what's proper—even at midnight—and a few more who disturb the NBC network sales department's taste as to what's proper at any time, the *Tonight Show* has been semi-fearless in choosing guests and subjects. It's showcased blatant sexists, underground warriors, ecologists, bigots, prison reformers, bomb builders and bomb throwers, politicians with their Reds, dietitians with their greens, integrationists with their blacks and singers with their blues.

"Carson is a man of conscience and good intentions who knows he has two obligations," commented an NBC spokesman. "His first obligation is to keep his show going. Then, his second obligation is to showcase some of these important subjects."

So the thinkers, the dreamers, the out-and-doers are buried in the midst of a club (act) sandwich between Joey-Jerry-Jackie comics and Peggy-Patty-Kathy starlets and eight weeks at the Blue Angel, six days at the Fairmount, and a Bar Mitzvah at the Villa Capri.

Steve Allen, along with Pat Weaver, started the but-seriously-folks part of the late night television shows. When he moved to Sunday evenings from his late night *Tonight Show*, he wanted to turn part of his prime-time program over to discussions of nuclear war, capital punishment and mental health. The Chrysler Corporation, sponsors of that program, put their thumbs down on NBC salesmen, who put their thumbs down on the programming department, who put their thumbs down on the engineers, who put their thumbs down on the switches that could send that kind of show out to televisionland.

But other than good conscience or good programming why should the late night television shows—the *Tonight Show*—

turn time over to people who clear their throats a lot while they try to clear up their subject matter?

Nobody took pen in hand or pique in tone to demand that Ed Sullivan have Dr. Jonas Salk and his vaccine team on stage. No newspaper columnists demanded Red Skelton follow his Guzzler's Gin act with panelists from Alcoholics Anonymous or that Bob Hope field three North Koreans or that Lawrence Welk break bubbles with a non-sudsing ecologist.

These people and their performances were intended as pure fast-acting, permanent-press entertainment. Nobody expected —or even wanted—them to carry a message to Garcia or Jackson, Wong, Johnson or Smith.

Those were the days of television's adolescence, say the critics. Now that it's grown up it has a responsibility to give us something as valuable as the valuable time it demands and takes.

But facts show that a program dedicated to the discussion of nuclear war can kill off more viewers than three H bombs.

Urban housing discussions can clear more rooms than a wrecking ball.

Our dwindling-natural-resources can turn out more television sets than a power blackout from New York to Davenport, Iowa.

But so can Joey-Jerry-Jackie.

Patty-Peggy-Kathy.

Doctor-doctor-doctor.

Three weeks at the Copa—two weeks at the Royal Box— eight days at the Concord.

And now one hundred fifty-two words-per-minute from the sponsor.

The *Tonight Show* could add important material.

Where late night's yellowing light has shone its brightest is in an area which the talk show producers seem to overlook the most.

Not the massive, doomsday subjects that sit as heavily on the viewer's head as a full-house pizza sits on his stomach.

And not the lightweight one-liners of heavy-handed comics.

But somewhere in between seems to be the truth.

Every once in a while the *Tonight Show*—and other talk formats—have found pure, joyful communication.

A cab driver who talked about getting a cab in the rain.

A bellhop who gave inside information on hotel tipping.

A used-car salesman with tips on out-tricking dealers.

The people-who-know about dieting, about love-making, about child-rearing, about job-finding, about smart-buying, pet care, and the thousand and one day-in-day-out problems of just surviving have been the most consistently popular guests on the late night talk shows.

Pat Weaver established the late night format as a "magazine" format.

Broadway Open House was a combination of *Police Gazette* and *Mad*.

Steve Allen turned it into *Billboard*, *Downbeat* and the *Saturday Review*.

Jack Paar changed it to *Reader's Digest* and *True Confessions*.

And Johnny Carson's version is a cross between *Playboy* and *TV Guide*.

Along the way, the *Tonight Show* has missed the most obvious magazine format—the service magazine. These are the "how-to," the better-way-through," the "ten-ways-toward" magazines which help themselves survive by helping their readers to survive.

According to publishers' earning statements, these are the only magazines which are healthy and happy and prospering these days.

They are based on the simple idea that you need help with your problems more than you need a laugh. That life is earnest and not Jerry-Joey-Jackie. That the word "Communication" is spelled with a *u* right in the middle of it.

If the *Tonight Show* went into a service magazine format, the show would go something like this:

"How I killed them in Vegas" would be replaced by how to keep your kids from being killed by street gangs.

"My three weeks at the Americana" would be replaced by how to find a job.

"My swimming-pool-and-tennis-court Beverly Hills home" stories would give way to ten lowest-crime, least-expensive places in this country to live.

Do eight million, ten million, twelve million people a night really want to hear Henny Youngman play the violin again, hear Robert Clary do a medley of his 1952 hit again, watch Sammy Davis talk Yiddish again, look at Zsa Zsa's multiple chins with diamond place markers again?

Or would they open one eye—or, praise be, even both—if someone-who-knew turned to the camera and talked about: how to get a table in a sold-out restaurant, how to get better mail service, where to find good and cheap dentistry, how to save a twenty-dollar bill every time you go grocery shopping, the cheapest ways to fly, how any family can find buried treasure or some other form of a better-life-through-television.

Sort of a *Sesame Street* for adults.

Educational television for things-as-they-could-be instead of as they are.

The *Tonight Show* could even add small, sensitive touches. . . .

. . . The *Tonight Show* goes off the air with a glare of lights, a bang of drums, a nudge of ribs, a wave of guests and a clap of hands. The last words of the day, for millions of Americans, are not the Twenty-third Psalm from the Bible, or Polonius' advice to his son from Shakespeare, or a hymn to Mom from Edgar Guest but a word from the apple corer man who has only ninety-nine of them left and the number in New Jersey is Nutley 2 . . .

Maybe, after eighty-nine minutes of mouth marathon

every night, the proprietors of the *Tonight Show* might consider giving sixty seconds to a thought-out thought for tomorrow. An idea from Santayana, some philosophy from George Bernard Shaw, a musing from Al Capp, a benediction from Satchel Paige—could give America something to sleep on besides stories about Sam Goldwyn.

There are other communications the *Tonight Show* could get into. It could give more time to the Bruce-David-Mark young comics and less to the Jerry-Joey-Jackies. It could get out of the studio—the way Steve Allen and Pat Weaver wanted to—and bring the audience scenes from plays, dances from ballets, arias from operas, fast-breaking news as it happens. It could show more film and videotape of foreign entertainers or the Miss Nudist beauty contest or ten-minute student and art films which win awards all over the world and which are never seen by Americans.

The *Tonight Show* could experiment with and develop electronic humor—the kind Ernie Kovacs and Steve Allen and Dave Garroway created and which was dropped when the network accountants found that people would watch radio with pictures.

The *Tonight Show* could use its time and its talents and its audience to examine mental telepathy and extrasensory perception and suggestive healing and the laying on of eyes, or other experiments to find out if communication is actually our most important human endeavor.

At one end, it could run national lotteries to raise money. And at the other, it could inform and educate to raise good citizens. It could fulfill television's aborted destiny as the meeting ground for men and minds: you and your universe. And it could be done with a sense of humor and national excitement.

Instead, what we have is a chatterbox-equipped night light.

Joey-Jerry-Jackie.

Metro-Warners-Universal.

Roxy-Palace-El Tinge.

Statler on the second, the Sahara on the thirteenth, the College Inn on the twentieth.

A week in Dallas, three days in New York, and twenty years on NBC.

Batting the breeze, shooting the bull, chewing the fat.

While the clock ticks its rounds and it grows later and later.

For the dream that was Pat Weaver's.

And the promise that was *Tonight.*

And for the fraying, mildewed miracle of television itself.

HUMOR THROUGH THE YEARS

TONIGHT—A STEVE ALLEN MONOLOGUE

HOW TO HAVE FUN ABOARD SHIP

STEVE:

The first thing to do is to get
acquainted with some of the other
passengers. Here's the best way to
do it: As soon as you board the
ship, move into the wrong stateroom.

Next, unpack carefully. Make sure
you don't break any of the bottles.

The first day out is the best day
to make friends. The best way to
make friends, is to roll the Captain,
and wear his uniform around the
ship.

To avoid the bother of tipping the
steward during the trip, tip him on
the first day. Tip him right over
the rail.

There are many games to play aboard
ship . . . and you'll love them . . .
games like Shuffleboard, Backgammon,
Trap shooting, and one game that
everybody loves, called, "Man Overboard"
. . . Whoever's left at the end of the
trip, wins.

If things get dull after a few
days out, and the weather's foggy

and miserable, here's a great way
to have fun. Sneak into the
Captain's Bridge, hold a popsicle
up in front of his binoculars and
yell, "Iceberg Ahead!"

If that doesn't work, try this:
When everybody's asleep, open any
stateroom door quietly, pour in a
bucket of water, and yell, no time
for pajamas, we're sinking fast.

A typical Paar monologue as supplied by longtime Paar writer, Walter Kempley.

JACK PAAR SHOW 1958

ET CETERA

Good evening – welcome to the show. I
think you'll have a lot of fun tonight –
we discovered a new method to help you
laugh – just one word of caution —
please, no one light a match while the gas
is in the theater. . . . .

We have some interesting people on the show
tonight—
Needleman, the human fly, will perform for
us—he will, that is, if he recovers from
the DDT a near-sighted stage hand sprayed on
him. . . . .

Harvey Hammershlag, a bank teller, will be here
to give short lecture on Bank Swindlers—
it'll be a short lecture because his plane
for Brasil leaves at 1:15. . . . .
- -
And here is Picadilly Peyton Place, Hermione
Gingold. . . .
And here is the John Barrymore of Pantomime
Quiz, Hans Conried. . . . .
- - - - - - - - - - - - - - - - - - -
- - - - - - - - - - - - - - - - - - -
We have a geisha girl on the show tonight –
she'll sing "Kimona My House."

We in America buy a lot of things made in
Japan – in a geisha house, do you ever turn
over a tea cup and find—made in Scranton,
Pa.???

All I know about geisha girls I learned
in the movie, "Teahouse of the August Moon"—
and that wasn't too much because I couldn't
understand Marlon Brando's Japanese accent. . . .
(I can't understand his American one. . . .)

We have geisha girls in America — only
we call them bartenders. . . . .

When you go in a geisha house, you take off
your shoes—you end up with a cup of tea
and a cold.
- - - - - - - - - - - - - - - - - - - -
Our director has a new drink – a very dry
martini—he calls it a Fresh martini —
because you put the vermouth in a Fresh roll-
on deodorant bottle and roll it across the
gin. . . . . .

A typical Carson monologue as supplied by longtime Carson writer, Walter Kempley.

JOHNNY CARSON '64

MONOLOGUE

Thank you – I'd blow you a kiss but I heard
about an entertainer who did that and fell
in love with his hand. . . . .

Welcome to the Tonight show – NBC's thorn
in its side. . . . .

I'm Johnny Carson. . . . . I say that only because
I heard a lady say: I thought the Lone
Ranger always wore a mask. . . . .

The city is going to spend 30 million to
clean the subways. It breaks down like this –
four dollars for a broom and the rest for
protection. . . . .

The subways are rather dirty. They look
like the inside of a barbecue pit. . . . .

Khrushchev has reported he has the ultimate
weapon. We've retaliated – we've given
all the western countries our answer –
Diner's Club cards. . . . . .